To Christopher
all the best
Edinburgh 19/11/7+
George [signature]

Songs of the Grey Coast

——————●——————

The Gold of Kildonan

Songs of the Grey Coast

——————●——————

The Gold of Kildonan

George Gunn

Chapman Publications
1992

Published by
Chapman
4 Broughton Place
Edinburgh EH1 3RX
Scotland

The publisher acknowledges the financial assistance of the
Scottish Arts Council in the publication of this volume.

A catalogue record for this volume is
available from the British Library.

ISBN 0-906772-44-3

Cover design & artwork by Fred Crayk
Photographs by Glenn Collett

Printed by
Mayfair Printers
Print House
William Street
Sunderland
Tyne and Wear

Foreword

George Gunn is a writer with an intense feeling for place. Not only for the landscape, the wildlife, the weather of a place, but also, and above all, for the people. He glories in the differences between cultures. He relishes the richnesses specific to a community, in its everyday particulars of living, in the language of its people in home, pub and street, and in the shared, formative experiences of that community, past and present.

He grew up on the far north of Scotland, in Caithness, and it is a great pleasure to those with a love for the low-lying Pictlands north of Dingwall to see him join the ranks of Neil Gunn, Donald Campbell and a very few others in working in the language and story of the people of what Neil Gunn has called 'The Grey Coast'. The Gaels have made a great deal of their ancient language and their mountains, and so they should; the North-East and the Doric have been championed and chronicled, quite rightly, further north, George Mackay Brown has put the Orkney Islands back on the literary map. Now George Gunn and the new Grey Coast Theatre Company, based in Helmsdale, launched with the premiere of *Songs of the Grey Coast*, are bidding fair to continue into the next century the celebration, which Neil Gunn began so gloriously in his novels, of that thin strip of fertile land that stretches up the north coast of the Moray Firth, past the inhospitable cliffs of the Ord and northwards until it opens out into the grateful flat lands of Caithness itself. There is much there to celebrate, and much that is too little known to the rest of Scotland, and the rest of the world.

In his poems, George Gunn captures with a sharp eye a succession of images from his life, from his childhood and ongoing complex relationship with family and home turf in Caithness, to his experiences as a roughneck on the oil rigs offshore, to Glasgow and far beyond. The images in the poems are of a more personal, emblematic kind, reaching out through his memory of a grandmother towards larger statements of human values, taking a childhood experience of being dragooned into waving a flag at passing 'royals' as a jumping-off point for a vehement rejection of the social structures they underpin.

Like many a poet before him, he has clearly felt the need for the broader canvas of theatre to expand his images into small worlds, to set communities in motion through time, to explore a form in which words still carry the weight, but in which human character, social conflict, and the larger issues of society like justice an class are tangible presences.

He wrote several plays before the two in this volume, notably for George Byatt's PKF company, a group which shared his passionate and flamboyant socialism, and his relish for words. However in the two plays in this volume, he is moving into a vein of more confident exploration of community and place. In them we can find all his voracious appetite. for the detail of history, for the rhythms of the English language as spoken in the north, for the feel of the way the mind moves. Here also are the unspoken consequences of the interplay between humanity and the elements, the effects on human character, good and bad, of the harsh struggle with the land and the sea. And here is his sense of the great historical injustices wrought in this area by a privileged few upon the disempowered many: crimes which are still not put right today.

It was a terrific pleasure to be at an early performance, in Helmsdale, of the Eden Court company's production of *The Gold of Kildonan*. It was good to feel the joy of that audience seeing a part of their own story rescued from oblivion, giving some value to their past, some dignity to their present, and a context for moving into the future. I look forward to being in Helmsdale once again for the production of *Songs of the Grey Coast*, and to the start of a new theatre company. May they fare well, and stick to their Gunns. And may George continue to explore the richnesses of human life, and of language, and of theatre.

John McGrath
September 1992

Songs of the Grey Coast

First performed by

Grey Coast Theatre Company

at

Kildonan Hall

20th October 1992

Seoras Swanson.. Matthew Zajak

Shona Henderson..Eliza Langland

Marni Swanson ....Joy McBrinn

Henry Henderson... Gordon Neish

Moira Swanson .... Lucy McCarra

Struan Cheyne ....Colin Brown

Dr Brian Blacksmith...Michael Derrington

Director..Hugh Loughlan

Set Design...Fred Crayk

Music.. Andy Thorburn

Lights... Peter Scott

Costumes .... Christine Ross

Stage Manager .... Paul Murphy

Deputy Stage Manager.. Peter Gordon

Assistant Stage Manager..James Warbrick

Administrator.. Catherine MacNeil

Songs of the Grey Coast

Cast

Seoras Swanson: Aged 33, son of the late Hector Swanson, works offshore in the North Sea.

Shona Henderson: 31, daughter of the late Hector Swanson. She is an artist.

Marni Swanson: Younger sister of the late Hector Swanson, in her late fifties, a farmer.

Henry Henderson: Aged 35, Shona's husband, an art teacher.

Moira Swanson: 28, Seoras's wife. We never really find out what she does.

Struan Cheyne: The local sheriff and gentleman farmer, in his mid-sixties.

Dr Brian Blacksmith: A nuclear physicist, in his mid-forties.

Set

The play takes place in the kitchen of the Swansons' farmhouse, two miles outside the village of Bunillidh, on the far north-east coast of Scotland. The time is the spring of 1991

for Lesley

Act I

"Going home.."

*As the lights come up we see the interior of a farm kitchen. It is a simple yet functional place. There is a table and four chairs in front of a Raeburn. On two of the chairs sit **Marni Swanson**, the farmer and **Struan Cheyne**, the local Sheriff. They both have large glasses of brandy in their hands. On the table sit two bottles of brandy, one empty and one freshly opened. **Cheyne**, who has his feet up on the fireguard, is a plumpish man with a posh anglo-Scottish accent and an arrogant air. He is used to being listened to and to being right. After all, as he says himself, he is the Sheriff. **Marni Swanson** is a sinewy, masculine-looking woman with a weather-beaten face and short combed-back hair. She is dressed in dungarees with a leather belt tied round the middle. They are laughing at some joke. **Marni** rises and goes over to the window which is extreme stage-left.*

Marni: I swear, Struan, ye're gettin worse.

Cheyne: I have every ambition.

Marni: Ye'd better watch yersel, boy, or wan day yer luck willna hold.

Cheyne: Luck? Luck, my dear Marni, has nothing to do with it. I am the Sheriff.

Marni: Just so. (*she drinks*) The only luck I've ever known is what I've hewn frae the ground wae my own two hands.

Cheyne: (*suddenly solemn*) This is hard land, an no mistake. But, my good woman, you were born to it. Your father, and his father, they kicked this land in the guts all their days.

Marni: (*she downs her drink*) Ach, but what d'ye ken on it? Ye walked straight intil yer fortune. Never had til lift a hand.

Cheyne: My dearest Marni, I own one thousand acres. It does not work itself.

Marni: Exactly. Yer wife works it. Ye sit on yer arse an throw the Tinks in jail for stealin the lead aff the kirk roof.

Cheyne: Well, I *am* the Sheriff. Are we to allow anarchy to run loose up and down the coast?

Marni: Anarchy, Struan, the only anarchy I've ever seen here is yersel tryin to get intil yer car after a good night on the drink. I've never locked the front door o this hoose in my life. Come on, man, admit it – there's nothin for ye til do here. Drunken drivin. Weekend fights in Bunillidh efter the pubs close.

Cheyne: Without a figurehead such as I this society would fall to pieces.

Marni: (*she moves back over and pours herself another drink*) Ach, Struan, ye make the law up as ye go along.

Cheyne: I like to think I have a little flair.

*   **Marni** *moves to the window.*

Marni: Ah but listen til that wind. There's rain ahind it. Fine weather for the lambing, eh? I widna be surprised if there's a bit o snow ahind the rain too. I've got four hunder sheep on the hill right now. The last thing I need is til be diggin ewes oot o snow drifts. No wae what's happened.

Cheyne: Trying times. Trying times. Hector will be sorely missed.

Marni: All I need at my age is a soakin. I'm no lek ye, Struan, I canna afford til pay a shepherd to do my dirty work for me. I've got the bank on one shoulder an all these damn feel rules an regulations on the other. A shepherd? I can hardly afford sheep feed!

> **Marni** *returns to her seat and the brandy.*

Cheyne: Fiddlesticks! You love tramping across the moor with a ewe under your armpit. All this guff about a hard life. You only do it to show your, well your...

Marni: (*interrupting*) Ay, my what? Oot wae it!

Cheyne: Well, your superiority over any man.

Marni: I'm better than any man. Any!

Cheyne: Of that I have no doubt.

Marni: I pay the men who work for me damned weel, an they ken it.

Cheyne: Quite. So why do they always leave?

Marni: I work them hard for their wages. An hard work doesna find many takers. No these days.

Cheyne: It couldn't be something else, could it?

Marni: Like what? (*pause*) Ye mean that I'm a woman? D'ye think it's never crossed my mind? Every day, every hour it's wae me.

Cheyne: It is unusual for a woman to run a farm. Especially here.

Marni: Yer wife runs yers, doesna she?

Cheyne: Quite so, dear girl, but she doesn't drive the tractors, plough the fields and clip the sheep like you.

Marni: More fool her then. More fool me. (*pause*) Sometimes I curse the day I was born a woman. It's a lonely world amongst these weaklins an cheats. I drive my men hard, I'm no denyin it. But I ask them til do nothin I willna or couldna do mysel.

Cheyne: That's precisely my point. Why bother with hired men if you can do it all yourself? Case proven. Next!

Marni: Oh, ye think ye're so smart! I had til work this place or it would've gone til ruin years ago. My two brothers were as much use as two hands short.

Cheyne: You never learned man management, Marni. It's a wonder anybody worked here at all!

Marni: Two useless brothers I had. Two excuses for men, who, who...

Cheyne: (*rising*) Who would rather have a quiet life with their wives an children than to be bullied an blackmailed by you!

Marni: What d'ye ken o it? What?

Cheyne: I know that they're both dead, prematurely in my opinion. I also know that you are in a pretty pickle and in your situation it is not wise to bawl and shout at me, because I am the Sheriff!

Marni mimics "I am the Sheriff". There is a pause and they both laugh and relax. Marni returns to the table and pours them both a large measure.

Cheyne: You may not believe it, but the Romans invented brandy to buy off the Gallic Celts and keep them soused. Nothing much changes think I. (*he drinks*)

Marni: Ye're right. I dinna believe ye.

Cheyne: Quite right, old girl.

Marni: (*in a temper but with obvious affection*) An I'm no yer ould girl either!

Cheyne raises his hands in mock horror, then slumps back in his seat.

Cheyne: Hector's funeral is tomorrow, Marni. Seoras and Shona will be arriving first thing in the morning I expect. Everything is going to come to a head.

Marni: Dinna I just know it. They'll be wantin their share o what's left. Neither o them ken anythin aboot this place anymore. They've been away in the sooth too long.

Cheyne: But they're still Swansons, and you can be sure they'll speak their minds sooner or later.

Marni: But what does it matter what they say? They can go til hell! This place is mine. I worked it. I made it what it is. Nobody can take it away from me, ye hear me? Nobody!

Cheyne: I hear you. But I've also read Hector's will. When your elder brother James died childless, he left his third to Hector, his wife having died previously. Hector in his turn left his two-thirds to Seoras and Shona. Whether you like it or not you are a legal minority.

Marni: This land is mine. My sweat an labour hev been ploughed intil the very ground. Nobody has the right.

Cheyne: Morally, maybe not. But legally, they have you.

Marni: (*blackly*) Never!

Cheyne: (*getting out of his seat*) Marni, I admire your stoicism, but you're not making sense. You know the way agriculture is going here in the north. You've wrestled hard with adversity these last years trying to make it work. God knows I've watched you change this place from a mixed beef and arable concern to a barley cash crop with your links land stuffed with sheep. Well, what happens? The bottom falls out of the European grain market and your sheep aren't worth the wool that keeps them warm.

Marni: My faither left me this farm on trust. Ye'll never understand.

Cheyne: The farm was passed down in equal thirds. You are only one third.

Marni, in a fit of temper, throws her brandy glass onto the Raeburn where it smashes spectacularly. There is a brief explosion of yellow flame. She half-screams, half-groans, and sinks down into her chair.

Marni: (*to herself*) Who'd be a dog in days lek these?

Cheyne: (*after a pause*) I know it's none of my business, but have you told Seoras and Shona about Dr Blacksmith?

Marni: What's it til do wae them? This place isna theirs yet!

Cheyne: Hector is dead. He's lying at peace in the front room. They are his surviving children and his heirs. Dr Blacksmith is working for the Nuclear Authority. Dammit, what he's doing here is a serious business!

Marni: I ken fine what business he's on. He's surveyin.

Cheyne: We both know what he's surveying for, don't we?

Marni: We do not!

Cheyne: You can shut your eyes and ears to it if you like. That's what they've paid you for! You know fine what they're up to.

Marni: (*rising aggressively*) Look here, Struan, ye may be a man an I may be a woman, but I swear I'll knock that fat face o yers oot the back o yer head!

Cheyne: (*whispering, almost a hiss*) No doubt, old girl. No doubt.

Marni: I'm no yer old girl!

> *Pause. Enter **Dr Brian Blacksmith**, a demure yet rather shy English nuclear physicist. He is neatly dressed in a dark, sober suit. He is also neat in his manner, and couples this with the nervousness of the scientist. He wears glasses which he takes off and puts on at various intervals during the following scene. He speaks with a well-educated English accent which is not pukka but yet his natural speaking voice.*

Blacksmith: I'm sorry. I was working on a report and fancied I heard some voices.

Marni: Ye did.

Cheyne: We were arguing, as usual.

Blacksmith: Oh, it's just that it was late, and I wondered...

Marni: (*more of a command than an offer*) Ye'll hev a dram.

Blacksmith: Eh, no thank you. I've got to finish this report.

Cheyne: (*takes **Blacksmith** by the arm and leads him to the table*) My God, man. That was not a request.

> *Marni goes to a cupboard and produces another glass, pours a measure and hands it to **Blacksmith**.*

Marni: Come intil the body o the kirk, boy. Drink up now. Ye look lek ye could use it.

Blacksmith: Thanks.

Marni: Slainte mhath!

Cheyne: Here's mud in your eye.

Blacksmith: Cheers.

> *They all drink. Then there is an awkward pause.*

Cheyne: So, doctor, have you had a good day at the harvesting?

Blacksmith: Harvesting? (*then understands*) Oh. Well, today was the first day of the seismic surveying. The preliminaries are complete, which is why I have to finish this report. Everything seems to be going smoothly, but it's too early to say anything – if that's what you mean?

Marni: Never you heed what he means. The Sheriff is a nosey ould souse. He's spent too long in that court o his where he's king that he thinks everybody should reveal everythin at his royal command.

Cheyne: Can a man not take an interest in the destiny of his native heath?

Blacksmith: The surveys will last for another two weeks at least. Then we go away and analyse them. It's all a lengthy process, I'm afraid. Quite boring, I imagine, to the non-scientific.

Cheyne: But we're all scientists here, doctor.

Marni: Dinna listen til the ould windbag. He's enough til confuse Confucius hissel.

Cheyne: But we are! The doctor here, of course, is a nuclear physicist, splitting atoms at every turn. Keeping the world safe for democracy. Tiny universes parting at his request.

Blacksmith: Hardly.

Cheyne: My dear chap, you are too modest. As for myself I delve into the murky science of the criminal mind. The black and white of the human psychology. It is, my dear doctor, the science of the labyrinth.

Marni: The only labyrinth ye've ever been in is dodging yer income tax.

Cheyne: (*ignoring her*) Then there is Marni here, a scientist of the fields and all their husbandries. Hers is the science of coax and persuasion. Hers is the science of the very earth itself. So, don't you see? We are all joined!

Marni: All I see is that ye're pissed.

Blacksmith: I see the holistic logic of your argument, Sheriff, and I must say I find myself agreeing. Very attractive indeed. Yes, I suppose we are all aspects of the one thing.

Cheyne: Exactly! The whole gestalt, if you'll pardon my German.

Blacksmith: That's very interesting, especially when you consider nuclear physics. Everyone thinks it some strange religion practised by men with bald eggheads, but physics is interconnected to everything else. What I do is as important to the future of the human race as the crops you grow, the sheep you breed.

Cheyne: Are leukaemia clusters important to the future of the human race, doctor?

Blacksmith: There is no evidence to link the reactor with the leukaemia cases in Bunillidh.

Cheyne: With all due respect, doctor: my foot!

Marni: My God, Struan, hev these anti-nuclear bourachs been gettin til ye?

Cheyne: As the Sheriff with more appeals in the High Court than any other in legal history I think that proves I have a mind of my own.

Marni: Ye've hardly got a pair o breeks that are yer own. So haud yer wheesht an hev anither dram. I lek ye better when yer blaizin.

She pours him another drink. **Cheyne** *is getting noticeably sozzled, but for the moment he's holding it well.*

Blacksmith: (*sadly*) I wish, for once, I could talk to someone up here without getting into an argument about nuclear power.

Marni: Pay no heed, doctor, although it's hardly surprising considerin oor history.

Blacksmith: I know you've had the reactor here for over thirty years and that it's a research and development prototype and not a producing power station.

Cheyne: No lightbulb in the north has ever known a volt from that place.

Marni: Struan, yer lightbulb fused years ago.

Blacksmith: And I know a lot of people think that the only reason that it was located up here was the distance from the centres of population.

Cheyne: So that if anything when wrong, so what? A few dead teuchters and a lot of dead sheep.

Blacksmith: That was never the way the authority looked at it.

Marni: We farmers hev had til live wae the nuclear reactor since day one, an it hesna affected us a bit. If it wisna for the jobs the reactor provided this place wid be a wasteland.

Cheyne: You've obviously never been in the Sheriff Court first thing on a Monday morning. I see a wasteland at the beginning of every week.

Marni: My God, Struan, I do believe ye're developin a bleedin heart.

Cheyne: On the contrary, I am still a Tory.

Blacksmith: There is no reason why agriculture cannot co-exist harmoniously with nuclear power.

Cheyne: Maybe with nuclear power, there you might have a point. But what you're up to, doctor, is something else entirely, is it not?

Blacksmith: It is common knowledge what I and my team are here to do. We are taking seismic surveys.

Cheyne: So you say. You're going to build a nuclear dump here, aren't you?

Marni: Ach, Struan, gie it a rest, boy.

Blacksmith: Nothing of the kind is certain. Surveys are being taken at twenty different sites all over the country.

Cheyne: Come on, man. Give me the benefit of some intelligence. I've been seeing through advocates and lying solicitors for years. I put it to you…

Marni: "I put it to you". Wid ye listen til the gowk?

Cheyne: (*half smiling, half serious*) I put it to you, that to alleviate the impending run-down of the nuclear plant along the coast there, which, as you have said, is research and development, which in this political climate is a favourite thing to be cut, your Authority plan to soften the blow by siting a reprocessing plant at the reactor. The bait being construction and servicing jobs, both of which, as you know doctor, fall into the "iffy" category. And in sheer numbers can no way match the amount of expected redundancies.

Blacksmith: That is not my field. I know nothing about it.

Cheyne: Well, it's common knowledge along this coast, doctor. But what isn't widely known – and here being a member of the Rotary Club is a great advantage – is that nuclear waste from all over the world is to be shipped here, treated here, and dumped here! Which brings us back to the sheep and teuchters scenario. (*to **Marni***) There's not going to be much of a market for your grain and mutton then, Marni, old girl. As to the fishing, well you can forget about that as soon as you like!

Blacksmith: I am a scientist, not a politician.

Marni: An this is my kitchen, Struan, no the Hooses o Parliament.

Cheyne: I should say so. The brandy is much better here. (*he fills up his glass*) The last time I was in that accursed House the stuff tasted like some awful socialist from Blackburn or somewhere had passed it!

Blacksmith: I can assure you that if any reprocessing plant or storage facility were sited here it would be entirely safe. Despite what you think, Sheriff, we in the Authority *do* know what we are doing. There is absolutely no need for such alarmist rhetoric. It really doesn't get us anywhere.

Cheyne: I know rhetoric doesn't get us very far, but stigma stops us dead. I tell you this, doctor, site a nuclear dump here and you finish off the indigenous industries at a stroke. Ways of being that have struggled on for a thousand years. You see, I've been sentencing and fining these folk for decades and they're not the simple rustic children that southerners always take them for. Yet sometimes, I swear, I dismay in my heart at them and sometimes *for* them. Yet I know they wouldn't thank me or anyone for pity. And because of who I am and what I do they hate me. Oh, I can't say I blame them. I know inside myself, and as Marni keeps pointing out, that I'm not really needed here. You see, dear doctor, I too am an agent of an authority. This coast has no need for crown or state, just as it has no need for your nuclear dump! You see, good fellow, it's because I know how you feel that I feel confident to talk to you this way.

> *Cheyne* slumps rather drunkenly into his seat, a beatific grin on his face.

Blacksmith: Do you? I wonder.

Cheyne: I've seen the people of this coast suffer much over the years. War, unemployment, depression, emigration, alcoholism – you name it. I've seen them bear up and I've grown to respect them. Love them, even. Though that's a word alien to the vocabulary of the northerner and certainly foreign to sheriffs, I can tell you. But to bring this plague upon them, resilient as they are, may be the last straw.

Blacksmith: (*almost losing his temper*) I don't know how many times I have to say this, and I don't expect you to believe me, but what we at the Authority wish is for the good of the community and the nation as a whole. Nuclear waste has to be processed and stored somewhere. All I am involved in is trying to identify the best site. It is bound up with the rock formation and the water course. And even if the Authority did choose here as a site there would have to be a public enquiry before we could even apply for planning permission.

Cheyne: (*laughing as though he's just heard a great joke*) Public enquiry? My foot! Public enquiries don't mean a damned thing, doctor. I mean, dear fellow, we *are* talking here about the Scottish Office, an institution run by bureaucratic Titos who have no concern about public opinion or popular desires. Why the hell should they? They are only there to serve their ruling oligarchy. Public enquiries indeed! My dear fellow, I've served on public enquiries. I've had the stiff white men in their stiff blue suits come up to me on the quiet and deliver their stiff dictatorial memos. You will see to this. You will see to that. No, my dear doctor, public enquiries are so much smoke on the water.

Blacksmith: I find your cynicism difficult to understand. I mean you are a member of the establishment. I thought you'd be ...

Cheyne: (*almost barking*) What?! One of us?! Don't you see, that it is because I am a member of the so-called establishment that I know this. I tell you, my friend, ten minutes spent in the company of a bunch of High Court judges is enough to make you question your sanity! (*after a pause he gets up and goes over to the window*) Listen, doctor, you are a good man and I honestly believe you when you say what you have to say. But we are all pawns for some higher purpose. To watch this coast being destroyed by cynical planning or good intentions is enough to break my heart. I am that rare thing, I know – a Tory landowner with a guilty conscience. But for all my money and office I am a native of this land. It's destiny is my destiny.

Marni: Ye talk too much.

Cheyne: As usual, Marni, my old girl, you are absolutely right. (*to* **Blacksmith**) Goes with the job, you understand.

Blacksmith: (*getting up*) Well perhaps we could talk further at some other time, Sheriff. I'm afraid I have to finish that report and then be up at the crack of dawn. (*remembers the funeral*) I hope I can pay my respects to your good brother?

Marni: Dinna bother, he wisna worth it.

Cheyne: Of course ye can, doctor. The cortège leaves at two. (*to* **Marni**) You have a foul tongue, woman. Hector was a fine man.

Marni: A fine man? The bugger never did a hand's turn in his life.

Cheyne: That's not true! How can you say that of your own brother?

Marni: Because it's true. Because I hev no brothers!

They have forgotten **Blacksmith**, *who is confused enough anyway.*

Blacksmith: (*meekly*) Well, good-night both. I really must go up.

Cheyne: NONSENSE! One for the road, and then we'll all get some beauty sleep.

*Cheyne practically hauls **Blacksmith** back towards the table.*

Blacksmith: Not for me, thank you. I'm no drinker and I've had far too much already.

Marni: The man doesna want one, Struan, so why canna ye leave it at that? Ye never know when til stop. That's yer trouble.

Cheyne: (*lets **Blacksmith** go*) Oh, is it now?

Blacksmith: Well, good-night.

Cheyne: Good night, doctor.

Blacksmith exits almost at a run.

Marni: The boy'll never sleep a wink the night efter ye goin on til him like thon. An he's too pissed til write anythin. God, ye're a ruffian.

Cheyne: Oh really? I thought I was rather gentle with him.

Marni: All that trock aboot "stigma" an "destiny". Ye nearly had me believin ye.

Cheyne: Well, I told him what I believe, an what the folk know. He had a right to hear it.

Marni: My God, man, ye'll scare him away.

Cheyne: An then where will you be? That's what you really mean. God, the extent of your selfishness sometimes turns my stomach.

Marni: Weel, there's enough o it til turn.

Cheyne: (*patting his stomach*) One has to look the part, old girl.

Marni: I'm no yer ould girl!

Cheyne: (*downing his glass*) Well, I have to scoot. Have a morning court I can't get out of. Service here in the house at one, off to the cemetery at two – is that correct?

Marni: Ay, I suppose so. God, ye should know, ye arranged it all.

Cheyne: What exactly are you going to do?

Marni: Do? Me? I'm goin til do nothin.

Cheyne: I've a feeling that that isn't one of your options.

Marni: I'll decide that, thanks.

Cheyne: Yes, I suppose you will. (*he goes and looks out of the window*) My goodness, is this a taxi I see coming up the track?

Marni: That'll be one of they bastards, no doot.

Cheyne: You mean your nephew and niece?

Marni: Vultures.

Cheyne: My God, woman, they are your own blood!

Marni: Thieves!

Cheyne: Well, I'm off out the back door. Best to be gone before they arrive. See you tomorrow. Keep your chin up, old girl.

Cheyne exits.

Marni: (*through clenched teeth*) I'm no yer bloody ould girl.

Suddenly she springs into life. She goes over to the window and looks out. Then she rushes around the kitchen tidying up glasses, bottles etc. she puts some more peats on the fire, rearranges chairs etc.

*Enter **Seoras** and **Moira**. **Seoras** is weighed down with* *luggage which he dumps onto the floor. **Moira** is the worse for drink. He is tall and well-built and quite handsome, every inch a Swanson; confident, affluent and well-dressed.*

*   **Moira** is dark also, with long brown hair which is slightly dishevelled. She is dressed in a long coat and well-made dark dress underneath. Her face is handsome with high cheekbones. Her make-up has seen better days. She looks confused.*

Marni: Oh Seoras!

Seoras: Auntie Marni!

*They embrace. **Moira** leans gently against a wall.*

Marni: *(as if she is about to cry)* It came so sudden, Seoras. I wisna sure what til do, or where til find ye.

Seoras: It's okay, Marni, I got word.

Marni: So I see.

***Marni** looks him up and down, and is obviously pleased at what she sees. Then she notices **Moira**. Her face drops visibly.*

Marni: An this must be Moira.

***Marni** and **Moira** shake hands nervously.*

Moira: *(slightly slurred)* Hullo.

Marni: My, but ye're the fly one, Seoras. Gettin married an no even tellin yer ould auntie. The deil take ye, boy. Ye didna even tell yer ain faither!

Seoras: Ach, ye know how things were atween the pair o us.

Marni: Ay, I do. But come on in an get a warm at the fire. I've put some fresh peats on so it should be fine an hot.

She ushers them both to sit down. They sit.

Marni: That's better now I can see ye both. Ye'll no doot be needin a dram after yer journey.

Moira: Ay. Magic.

Seoras: No thanks, Auntie Marni. It's been a long day. I just got off the rig this mornin.

Marni: Still at the North Sea, eh Seoras? My, but it's good that yer mither's no alive til see ye wastin yersel oot there.

Seoras: Marni, please. I'm just in the door.

***Marni** ignores this rebuttal and turns her attention on **Moira** who is not bearing up too well.*

Marni: So, Moira, how did ye manage til snare this one?

Moira: *(not understanding)* Where's ma fuckin drink, eh?

Seoras: *(as if jabbed by electrodes)* Moira, that's enough! *(to **Marni**)* It's been a long journey. Ye know how it is. Moira's tired.

Moira: No I'm no. I'm just beginnin tae perk up. I didnae want tae come here. It's like goin tae the north pole. See that fuckin train, man it should be in a museum.

Marni: *(genuinely shocked)* I see. Weel, ye've certainly got a foul tongue in yer heid, lassie.

Moira: I'm no a fuckin lassie. I'm a wumman.

Marni: Weel then, ye'd better hev a dram.

Marni pours three large measures.

Marni: (*to Moira*) Here ye go. (*to Seoras*) This'll perk ye up.

Seoras takes it grudgingly. Moira takes hers greedily.

Seoras: Well, tanks.

Marni: Slainte mhath.

Seoras: Yer health.

Moira says nothing and drinks hers down in one. Marni looks on half in amazement and half in disapproval. Seoras seems to shrink physically and sips reluctantly from his glass.

Marni: (*suddenly overcome with grief*) Oh, Seoras, it came as a great shock to me, I can tell ye. I brocht him over here, after all he *was* born here, an I didna lek the thocht o him lyin in that hoose now that he was on his own.

Seoras: Ye did right, Marni. Ye did fine.

Marni: I hed til get him screwed doon. The fluid in his chest was bubblin up. No a pretty sight, I can tell ye.

Seoras: Dinna fear, it wis for the best.

Marni: So ye canna see him. I'm sorry. Ye do understan, dinna ye?

Seoras: Of course I understand. Dinna fret. We all kent faither hed a heart condition. The last time I saw him he looked better, although he'd aged a lot.

Marni: He was never the same since yer mither died, God rest her soul. Oh she was a lovely woman, Seoras, an I canna help but tell ye that I miss her badly. I wanted her til come over here towards the end, where I could keep my eye on her an see how things were goin. But he widna let her come. She wanted til. I know fine she did.

At this point Moira, who has fallen asleep some time earlier, starts to snore loudly. Seoras shakes her by the shoulders.

Seoras: Moira, for God's sake.

Moira grunts and stops for a moment.

Seoras: She's really tired. She's not used til travellin such great distances. She's never been north o Perth in her life.

Marni: Oh Seoras, where did ye get sic a craitur as that?

Seoras: (*in anger*) What d'ye mean? She's no always lek this! She's no been hersel o late. Her mither's been ill. It's upset her. But she's a fine an generous person normally! Ye'll see.

Marni: Will I?

Seoras: Ay ye will! Look, that was one reason I never told ye or Faither that we were gettin married. I knew ye'd both disapprove. That ye'd look doon yer long northern nebs at her. So it was better that ye didna know.

Marni: Ye might at least've given us the benefit of the doubt.

Seoras: I know fine what happens when ye give Swansons the benefit o the doubt! I wanted no squabblin nor arguments o any kind at my weddin. I wanted a nice quiet ceremony an that's what we had.

Marni: An Shona?

Seoras: Ay, both Shona an Henry were there. They were our witnesses.

Marni: Weel, at least some o oor blood was there.

Seoras: Ay, an none spilled, an that was fine.

Marni: Ye mustna think much o yer ould auntie?

Seoras: Dinna start that, Marni, ye know fine how fond I am o ye.

Marni: Oh I dinna doot it, my bouyag. I dinna doot it. But it doesna seem lek last week that ye were runnin aroond here helpin me wae the farmwork. Ye were good at it too. A natural wae the beasts. Ye should've been a vet. Ye should've stuck in at University, Seoras, an no got thrown oot lek ye did!

Seoras: I wasna thrown oot. I left!

Marni: It broke yer good mither's heart. Broke mine too.

Seoras: Listen, Marni. I talked til mither aboot it long afore she died. It was alright by her. She only ever wanted for me what made me happy. Dinna deny her that now that she's gone. As til yersel, weel, ye can think what ye lek. Ye aye hev.

Marni: Ye're hard on yer auntie, boy. Ye an yer sister are all that I've got left in the world.

Moira starts to snore again. Seoras shakes her again and she stops with a grunt.

Seoras: Anyway, never mind me. Faither, did he...

Marni: (*forgetting herself*) He was a thief!

Seoras: Marni! My faither's just died. I know ye two were always arguin, but for goodness' sake – the man's dead! How can ye talk like that?

Marni: I'm sorry, Seoras, I'm no mysel.

Seoras: It's okay, I understand. It's all so terribly sudden this. Tell me what happened, if ye can?

Marni: Weel, from what I can gather he was oot at the peat stack potterin aboot. The doctor hed telt him til take it easy. For him that wasna hard an he seemed to be doin away quite the thing. Jimmy Manson an his wee lassie was wae him. Just bletherin lek. Then for some reason the lassie got a splinter in her thumb, so yer faither takes her intil the hoose til attend til her. That's when it happened. As he wis treatin her his bonnet fell off. So he bent don til pick it up, an... oh, Seoras! (*she gets weepy*)

Seoras: (*moved*) It's alright, Auntie Marni, it's alright.

Marni: He never got up, Seoras, he never got up!

Seoras: (*comforting her*) Easy now, easy.

Marni: (*composing herself*) Weel, the lassie went screamin oot til her faither. Just by chance the district nurse happened til be in the manse next door, but by the time she arrived he'd gone.

Seoras: My God. (*pause*) At least it was quick. He would've made a terrible invalid.

Marni: Angina comes when it suits her. Ye can never be sure when she'll strike. But ye're right, it was as weel he kent no pain. The doctor reckoned he was dead before he hit the floor.

Seoras: (*groaning*) God!

Marni: That's yer Uncle Jimmy. Now yer faither. The hert, she took the pair o them.

Seoras: (*absent-mindedly strokes his chest*) So close together, too.

Marni: Just two years.

Seoras: It's cruel when ye think aboot it.

Marni: For sure, for they werna ould men. Yer faither was only sixty-two an Jimmy only sixty-four. But here the weakness in he men is the hert. Sooner or later they all seem til go that road. The light seems til hev poured from us lek milk from a jug.

> *Seoras, as if to free himself from his grief, moves from his aunt over to the window. He stands silent for a moment.*

Seoras: Whose is the Volvo ootside? The Sheriff's?

Marni: It belongs til Doctor Blacksmith. He's lodgin here a time.

Seoras: Doctor Blacksmith? Who's he?

Marni: He's surveyin the land aboot here. He doesna lek hotels an there's plenty o rooms in this hoose. So when they asked me if he could stay here for a bit I said 'fine'

Seoras: "They"? Who're "They"?

Marni: Dinna be making a fuss, Seoras. I'll tell ye all aboot it after the funeral.

Seoras: Who's the minister? Dinna tell me it's still ould Sinclair?

Marni: Who else? He's the only one there is, so what can we do? But I swear, there's more brains in sheeps' heid broth.

Seoras: I widna mind so much, but he's so bloody boring. Maybe we'll get lucky an he'll be struck by lightnin or somethin.

Marni: Oh I wonder when Shona's goin til come?

Seoras: Weel, it might be quite soon. There's a set o headlights just turned off the main road.

> *Marni rushes over to the window at a speed we have not seen her move at before.*

Marni: D'ye think that's Shona? D'ye think it could be her?

Seoras: It might be. There'll be Henry too, of course. Mustna forget about Henry.

Marni: I wish I could? Oh, Seoras, what on earth did she marry thon dope for?

Seoras: She loves him. Ye've got til respect that.

Marni: Ach, he just doesna seem the richt one for Shona, somehow.

Seoras: He's infatuated wae her, an he's good til her. He lets her get on wae her paintin an he doesna seem til mind that she doesna sell many o them.

Marni: I canna say I ever took til him. There's something fousty aboot the craitur.

Seoras: Oh dinna tell me: he's no good enough for oor Shona who's so special!

Marni: Weel, he's no, an she is! Shona needs someone til challenge her. Some chiel wae a spark o smeddum aboot them.

Seoras: Some "chiel" lek ye, ye mean?

There is a frosty silence as they both stare out of the window. ***Seoras*** *moves across to where* ***Moira****, who has started to snore again, is sitting. He picks her up like a sack of potatoes and throws her over his shoulder.*

Seoras: I suppose ye think Moira's no good enough either, eh? But ye're wrong. Ye'll see.

Moira *continues to snore.*

Marni: Weel, she's got a fine pair of lungs on her, I'll say that.

Seoras: (*moving off*) I'm goin til put her til her bed, then I'll be back doon til greet Shona an Henry.

Marni: That'll be grand. I've aired yer room. It should be comfortable enough.

Seoras: Thanks.

Seoras *exits.* ***Marni*** *moves from the window across to the table.*

Marni: Thanks for what? Sorrow an bad lambing weather, that's all we know. I swear my heart'll burst if I hev til carry on much longer! (*she pours herself a drink and downs it in one*) Oh, Mither I need ye now! Strength! Strength! Give me strength!

Enter ***Shona*** *and* ***Henry****.* ***Shona*** *is more slenderly formed than* ***Seoras*** *but there is still the distinctive look of the Swanson about her. She is very handsome with a strong face, deep brown eyes and long brown hair. To Marni she is the living image of her mother with whom she was in love.* ***Shona*** *is wrapped in a long white coat underneath which she wears jeans and a jumper. She wears her hair tied back with a red scarf.*

Henry *is some years older than* ***Shona****. He is tall and thin with a beard which, like his hair, is slightly ginger. Both are streaked with grey. This makes him appear much older than he actually is. He wears a tweed jacket and jeans, and is weighed down with cases.*

Shona *runs to her auntie and throws her arms around her.*

Shona: (*in a rush*) Oh Marni, Marni, what's happened here? We just got back from Tuscany, literally got into the flat an it was Seoras on the phone. I still can't believe it. We haven't stopped travelling for what seems like days. Oh, it's good to see you again! It's been too long. How are you? Where is he? I'm sorry. (*she bursts into tears*)

Marni: He's dead, my lambie, he's dead.

Shona: No. Tell me? Can I see him?

Marni: I'm sorry, it's too late. We hed til screw the lid doon. I canna tell
ye... (*through her tears*) My, ye look fine an bonny. Just lek yer
mither.

Shona: Faither, he...

Marni: Shoosh now. He met wae a quick end, yer faither. I'll tell ye all
aboot it in the morn. Safe til say he kent no pain. I canna think what
else til say. It was good o ye til make it. An so early. We werena
expectin ye til the mornin.

> *Henry moves over to join them.*

Henry: We thought the sooner we got here the better.

> *They shake hands awkwardly. Marni is awkward with most men,
> save for Cheyne and Seoras.*

Marni: Still, it's been a long drive for ye, Henry.

Henry: Oh, it wasn't so bad.

Shona: Is Seoras here?

Marni: Ay, an Moira. Although I'll doot if she kens it.

Henry: Is she...?

Marni: As fou as a partan.

Shona: Moira's a tortured soul. But there's good in her. What do we
know of people like Moira? Their lives are a mystery. We're over
protected in the north.

Marni: Are we Shona? I hevna noticed.

Henry: (*to Shona*) We've just arrived, darling. The lassie's not on trial.

Shona: Ay she is. Women like her are always on trial. But Seoras can see
the good in her, an so can I.

Marni: The soul o yer mither walks here when I hear ye speak.

Shona: (*confused, softly*) No.

Marni: She was a fine an beautiful thing, yer mither. A rare spirit, but
he bad used her, lek he bad used everythin else he touched.

Shona: Marni, no...!

Marni: There wasna anythin he widna use or waste. Be it money, or
trust, or yer lovely, lovely mither. It's better that he's dead.

Shona: (*shocked*) How can ye say such things? (*her northern accent
returns*)

Henry: (*holding Shona*) Come here, Shona. Marni is upset, can't ye see?
We all are. We should go up to our room an sleep.

Shona: (*upset*) No. We're just in the door. Marni, ye always were a
puzzle, but ye're my auntie none the less. What's got intil ye? I used
til play wae ye when I was a bairn. What's behind all these cruel
words? I canna believe ye mean them. I canna!

Marni: Ye'd better, for I do! Take Henry's advice an go up til yer bed.
Ye'll be needin yer sleep.

Shona: No! I willna go til my bloody bed!

Henry: Shona.

Marni: Still got yer temper, I see. Ye hevna changed much.

Shona: I hev. Oh ye dinna know how much. I know about light an dark, aboot shape an form. Aboot texture an perspective. Aboot art, Marni, aboot art!

Marni: I see that every day when I'm feedin the sheep.

> *Shona slumps into a seat.* **Henry** *moves behind her and rubs her shoulders gently.*

Shona: My faither's dead. Yer brither.

Henry: What the hell's wrong with you Swansons?

Marni: (*stares at him coldly*) There's nothin wrong wae us, save that oor blood gets thinner.

Henry: Blood? You're all good at blood. Aren't things bad enough?

> *Enter* **Seoras**

Seoras: Obviously no.

> *Shona springs to her feet and launches herself at* **Seoras** *who catches her and twirls her around. There is obviously a close bond between brother and sister.*

Shona: Oh Seoras!

Seoras: My wee lamb.

> *They embrace*

Marni: Take a look, Henry. True love.

> *Henry winces visibly*

Seoras: (*holding her at arm's length*) My, but the Italian air seems til suit ye. Ye've got a tan. Or is it just paint? (*he strokes her cheek to make sure*)

Shona: (*laughing*) Everybody thought I wis a Greek.

Seoras: (*laughing too*) I'm sure they did. (*he moves over to Henry*) Hey, boy, I'm glad ye could make it.

> *The two men shake hands eagerly.*

Henry: It was a bit hairy at times. The old Peugeot nearly packed in coming over the Storrie Hill. Sounds just like a Challenger tank now.

Seoras: Weel, ye made it anyhow. I just wish these were better circumstances.

Henry: It was a great shock.

Marni: Circumstances are an open prison, Seoras. When ye goin til realise that?

Seoras: (*sharply*) If ye'd lay off the drink then they might open up!

Marni: (*mockingly*) My wee lamb.

Shona: Why don't we all hev some tea? I'm dyin for a cuppa. Are there eggs, Marni? I'd just love some fried eggs. I'm starvin. There was nothin til eat north o Ardgay! D'ye still keep hens, Marni? Surely ye do?

Marni: (*happy again*) Of course I do. An ducks too. But they're gettin on. I'm sure that ould drake's over a hunder.

Shona: Then the scullery must be fill o eggs lek it used til be!

Marni: Mebbe no so fill. C'mon, I'll show ye.

Shona: I want big broon ones!

Marni: Then ye'll hev them, for there's no shortage o thon species.

Shona: Wae big yellow yokes lek the sun!

Marni: Just the very donkeys!

> *Marni and Shona exit arm in arm, laughing.*

Seoras: That pair are dangerous.

Henry: All Swansons together.

Seoras: D'ye think so. Marni sees my mither in Shona, an it's true she's gettin more lek her every day. Marni an my mither were … well, very close.

Henry: I know about Marni, Seoras, you don't have to disguise anything.

Seoras: Weel, that's a relief at least. If no foreign til a Swanson.

Henry: I'll miss Hector.

Seoras: Ay, me too.

Henry: He was like an encyclopaedia about the coast here. I learned a lot from him.

> *Seoras pours them both a drink.*

Henry: It's strange, but being in Italy, I thought for the first time that this country is finished. That no matter how hard she struggles to get up off the floor she keeps getting knocked back down again.

Seoras: Henry, Henry, ye're always philosophisin, eh?

Cheryne talks to Shona while Seoras looks on

Henry: I know it must be difficult to make sense of it all. I mean, you're out in the thick of it in the North Sea.

Seoras: D'ye s'pose that us roughnecks canna think? That we're slow simple bairns wae drillin mud for brains who need the story telt till them nice an easy?

Henry: No, of course not. I meant...

Seoras: I know what ye meant. I know fine what's goin on.

Henry: Don't get me wrong. It's just that it's such a waste. In Tuscany the folk seem to have so little. They're no better than crofters, an poor ones at that. Yet they are so rich.

Seoras: An ye think we're no?

Henry: Oh, we're rich alright, but we're bein hoodwinked. Ould Hector knew that. I've heard him talk about it often enough. You know, when we'd be up in the hill cuttin the peat.

Seoras: He'd gab all day up there. Used til drive us all nuts.

Henry: He just knew so much. I've never learned so much from one man.

Seoras: But he wisna just one man. He was a conglomeration o centuries. An I ken ye think the peat cuttin was nice an romantic. Til the rest o us it was slavery!

Henry: A day in the hill'll tame lions! That's what he'd say.

Henry: Like I said, he'd say a lot o things. God knows if half o it was true?

Henry: I know ye think I'm a bit o a hippy, Seoras, practically no better than a white settler, a Bongly! But I tell you, I'd live up here if I could.

Seoras: A lot o folk seem til agree wae ye. This coast is bein colonised. Damn me if ye can hear a local accent in the pub anymore.

Henry: Hector welcomed them. Do you?

Seoras: That ould goat'd talk til anybody. Prince or Tink, it was all the same til him. As long as it passed the time o day. Man he could talk the bleat oot o a flock o sheep.

Henry: He should've been recorded. It's all disappearing, Seoras, all those stories. Like mist off a sea loch. He was like a university.

Seoras: An the only qualification ye needed was a dram, or a spade til lean on. God, what peasants we are!

Henry: Why has history got to be like this? The carpets bein pulled from their feet! I see it every time I come north.

Seoras: Ay, but ye'll go sooth again. Death is the only lastin thing here, an the only place folk lek my faither are guaranteed a space. Ye dinna need money there. Nor ministers neither. Mebbe hell is bein aroond after the dead hev gone, lek here where the only thing that brings folk thegither are funerals. But I want life, Henry, life!

Henry: In Italy at least there's sunshine.

Seoras: An here? Here there's...

Enter Marni and Shona

Shona: (*triumphantly*) Eggs! Beautiful warm brown speckly eggs! Straight from their donors with love an good wishes. Hmmm, I can smell 'em from here!

Marni: Get the fryin pan, Seoras, dinna stand there lek a limmer!

> *Seoras goes and fetches the large cast iron frying pan from beneath the sink. He slaps it onto the Raeburn with a dramatic flourish. Laughing, Shona cracks egg after egg into the pan.*

Marni: Good girl. No fat. Grey coast eggs need no fat. Fry em up, Shona. Fry em up lek summer days!

Shona: Oh, I'll do more than that. I'll fry em up lek bloody eggs!

> *They all laugh as if they needed it for relief. Suddenly Marni collapses. Seoras catches her and gently lays her on the floor.*

Seoras: Hey, Auntie, take it easy.

Henry: Are you alright, Marni? Can I get you anything?

Marni: (*coming to*) No. I'm fine. Dinna fuss now.

Shona: Ye're lookin gey peely-wally, Auntie Marni. What's the matter?

Marni: It's my neck. It's no right.

Shona: (*bends over and feels gently the back of her neck*) Yer neck? How come?

Marni: Rheumatics. They're no sure. They're runnin tests. It's a long story, but it's been playin me up o late.

Seoras: What does the doctor say?

Marni: (*getting to her feet and sitting in a chair*) What does he no say. He just gies me pills.

Shona: Doctor Mackay?

Marni: Who else is there?

Seoras: Doctor Drams! It's a wonder the ould goat was sober enough til read the labels.

Shona: The man should be retired. I mean, he must be over seventy.

Henry: Maybe you should see a specialist, Marni. It's not that far to Wick.

Marni: (*spits the word out*) Wick! I widna go til Wick til see the Queen! An stop all this fashin! I hevna hed a day's illness in my life!

Seoras: Calm doon, Marni. Listen, ye're goin til hev til accept that ye're no spring chicken.

Shona: (*disapprovingly*) Seoras!

Marni: (*she pours herself a drink*) Oh I ken what ye're thinkin. Yer daft ould auntie's on the way oot. Time til stick her on the scrap heap. Time til send her off til Wick for 'tests' an more 'tests'! She's over the hill! Canna hack it anymore! (*she takes a big drink*)

Seoras: Not at all. All I meant was...

Marni: I ken fine what ye meant. But let me tell ye somethin, my fine young mannie. Big as ye are, an as ould as ye've got, ye're no too big or ould for a clap roond the lug!

Henry: (*to Seoras*) She seems to be recoverin.

Marni: The cheek o it! The worth o tuppence an the cheek o thruppence, that's aye been the way wae ye, Seoras. My God, what's that smell?

Shona: My eggs!!!

*She rushes over to the Raeburn where black smoke is pouring out of the frying pan. She grabs the handle which is very hot. She screams and drops the pan onto the floor. **Sheoras** and **Henry** burst out laughing. **Shona** then rushes over to the sink and puts her injured hand under the cold tap. She groans. The plumbing, being ancient, forces the water out of the tap with such a rush that she is soaked. She curses loudly.*

Shona: (*almost crying from pain and embarrassment*) That's right, laugh! Go on, laugh! Ha ha ha!!! That's men for ye!

Henry *moves over to her and starts drying her down with a towel.* **Seoras** *is on his knees trying to extinguish the smoke with a dish-towel.*

Henry: (*gently*) Calm down, darling, it's alright. Have you burnt your hand bad?

Shona: (*in a little girl voice*) Not really.

*A smile finds its way onto her face as **Henry** lovingly dabs at her hand with the towel.*

Marni: Slap some butter on it, that's the best thing. Seoras, stop flailin aboot there an makin even more o a mess. Go through an get some butter oot the press. Hurry now!

Seoras, *still laughing, does this. He exits.*

Shona: I'm sorry, Marni, I've wasted yer eggs. I'm sorry.

Marni: What's a few burnt eggs?

Shona *gets down on her knees and tries to tidy up the smoking remains.* **Henry** *sweeps it all up with a brush and shovel.*

Marni: Handy aboot the hoose, is he no? Come here, my poppet, an let yer ould auntie hev a look at ye.

Shona *moves over to **Marni**. At this moment we see the little girl in her. We can imagine the relationship they must have had when she was a child. **Shona** is full of trust and respect and looks fresh and young. **Marni** notices this and becomes very motherly and soft-sounding. This is as feminine as she will ever be.*

Marni: (*cradling **Shona**'s hand*) Hardly any damage done at all. My, but ye've got pretty hands, poppet. Just lek yer mither's. Beautiful an long. Ye look after them now.

Shona: Red hot fryin pans are no for me.

Marni: Indeed they are no, my troskie. That pan is oulder than ye an Seoras put thegither. (*sadly*) Everythin is gettin ould roond here. Seoras is right.

Shona: (*shocked*) Auntie Marni! Seoras is never right!

Marni: (*smiling*) Ye say that now?

*Enter **Seoras** with butter*

Marni: (*to Seoras*) Ye should hear what she's sayin aboot ye, boy.

Seoras: Oh I dinna want til know. It's always bad. Here's yer butter. Mebbe ye should rub some intil her head. It might activate a few brain cells. (*he holds his hand*) Danger! Danger! White-hot metal! Do not touch!

> *Marni takes the butter from him and applies it to Shona's hand. Shona scowls at Seoras.*

Marni: That's enough oot o ye, lad.

> *Shona sticks her tongue out at him and he puts his thumb to his nose. We see at this moment the 'lad' in Seoras. We also see, for the first time, the three Swansons together: the aunt, her nephew and niece as they must have been in their childhood days. They seem to be at ease with each other as if they are the only people in the world. One gets the feeling that they have finally come home, and for a moment the atmosphere of bereavement is lifted. Henry, having finished sweeping, watches them with a mild fascination. He feels excluded, yet content to see his wife among her people. When he speaks the spell is broken.*

Henry: (*at the window*) The wind seems to be droppin. The farmers might be able to keep their bonnets on tomorrow.

Seoras: (*joining him*) It'll be blowin squalls for the next two weeks. Seems til be the same every lambin time. Hailstones, rain an gales. Typical April weather. If there is a God he certainly doesna lek sheep.

Henry: Can't say I blame him.

Shona: How d'ye know it's a 'him'?

Seoras: Oh here we go! Shona the feminist! I wondered how long it wid take afore the beast emerged from its lair! Come on, then, let's all hear how God is a vegetarian single parent black woman!

Shona: Yer too far gone til bother wae, Seoras. I'm no goin til waste my breath arguin wae ye just for yer amusement.

Marni: Quite right, Shona. Never mind him. What do men ken aboot anythin anyway? There ye go. That's ye.

Shona: (*looking at her hand*) Thanks, Auntie, ye're wonderful.

> *Shona kisses Marni on the cheek. Marni is visibly moved by this as she is unused to intimacy. She puts her hand up to her cheek as if some deep memory has flashed its way through her mind.*

Shona: No, Seoras, ye're just part o the procrustian bed o chauvinism an male behaviour in general. It's yer cultural conditioning, poor lamb. An it's no even yer fault. Pitiful really.

Seoras: (*in mock surprise*) Ye mean, I'm no the new man?

Shona: Seoras, ye're no even the ould man.

> *Shona has moved over to the window and holds Henry from behind with tired affection. Marni watches them as if she were a visitor at the zoo. Seoras watches Marni.*

Marni: My, but it's grand til hev young folks aboot the place again. (*to Seoras*) Ye never come an see me enough. Yer poor ould auntie hes til make do wae her animals.

Seoras: It's a long way, Auntie Marni, an I'm on the rig half the time.

Marni: I know it's no easy for ye, Seoras, but yer sister doesna hev the same excuse.

Shona: Oh, Marni, I dinna need excuses. I'm sorry I dinna come til see ye as much as I'd lek, but we hev a busy life, eh Henry?

Henry: Oh ay, that we do. But I'll tell you, Marni, I'd be up here all the time if I had my way. This coastland is a paradise as far as I'm concerned.

Marni: Ay, ye're keen enough, Henry, I'll say that.

Henry: Especially this time of year. Spring an the beginnin of the lambin season. The great renewal. Nature restockin. Life goin on.

Marni: I've hed too many soakins til believe in that stuff. For me an for all farmers it's a time o worry.

Shona: Oh, Auntie Marni, ye worry aboot everythin!

Marni: An weel I might! God knows if I'll get a man for the lambin this year. It's difficult til get an experienced shepherd. The two lads I've got the now are fine enough but they're green ahint the lugs. No doot I'll hev til craik this sore ould neck aroond the hills an links this year again. I'll miss yer faither for that. He aye kept a weather eye on things.

Shona: (*suddenly bursting into tears*) I'll miss him too. So very much…

Henry holds her closer and cradles her head.

Henry: There now, my girl. Take it easy.

Shona: Oh Henry, I feel so sad.

Henry: I know, lover, I know. But be strong now.

Seoras: Tomorrow mornin, if ye lek, we'll go doon til the links, all o us an get some shochit eggs. Lek wae used til when wae were bairns. Mind how they used til swoop on us, eh Shona? Ye were aye frichtened, an when ye were really peedie ye used til squeal lek a wee piggie. (*he mimics a piglet squealing*)

Shona: (*through her tears*) I never did. Ye're makin it up as usual. An anyway ye always managed til get covered in coo cach!

Henry: It should be light aboot half six. D'ye think you could manage that, Shona?

Shona: (*groaning*) I suppose so. I dinna think I'll sleep much. No wae faither doon the stair.

Marni: I dinna think I'll sleep again.

Seoras: (*going over to Marni*) Ye need yer sleep more than anybody, Marni.

Marni: Oh I'll sleep soon enough. But there'll be no wakenin from that one.

Shona: (*breaking free of Henry*) Why hev ye got til speak lek that? Must we always be talkin aboot death? Is it no enough that Mither's dead, an now poor Faither? An both o them taken afore their time? We should be talkin aboot the future, aboot what we're goin til do wae oor lives! Aboot what's goin til happen here! Nobody seems til be interested!

Henry: You're tired, Shona. Don't get so excited. We're all upset.

Shona: Are we? I wonder.

Henry: What d'ye mean?

Shona: I mean that some o us are mebbe far from bein upset. Mebbe some o us are glad.

Henry: Shona, really you mustn't…

Shona: (*turning on him*) Oh Henry, ye're far too innocent. Ye dinna know the Swansons. Behind the front o compassion there's an Iago waitin til plot an scheme.

Seoras: Ach pack it in, Shona. Ye're talkin drivel!

Shona: Am I? (*up close to him*) D'ye really believe that?

Seoras: Ay! Now shut up.

Marni: No. Let her speak. Her Mither's no dead these past years when she's standin there lek that.

Shona: Why d'ye hev til go on aboot Mither lek that? I'm no her, Marni, I'm no! But lek me she could see through all yer plots an lies. There's never been one day when ye hevna been at each other's throats.! Faither, Uncle Jimmy an yersel. A triangular feud that seemed til go on forever. But two are dead now. Lek dogs over a carcass ye were. An the carcass was this place, this land, this grey coast. It drove Mither mad. Dinna ye see that yer constant bickerin and warrin drove her til it. So damned be the name o Swanson!

Shona sobs exhaustedly and Henry catches her as she sags.

Henry: Shoosh now, my angel. Take it easy. Don't be gettin yourself even more upset.

Shona: (*struggling to be free of his arms*) The Swansons only know death. They're born til it. It's their curse for bein alive. They're no human, but black hungry ghosts that hev visited this hoose. (*weakly*) Why do the black ghosts visit us? How many more in the world are there til come here? How many?

Enter Blacksmith, nervously.

Blacksmith: I'm sorry if I'm disturbing you all, but I think I've left my spectacles here in the kitchen. Have any of you seen them, I wonder? Oh, there they are on the dresser.

Blacksmith moves over to pick up his spectacles, and the four stare at him as if he were a ghost.

Blacksmith: I say, is there anything wrong? What are you all staring at me like that for? What is it?

Lights fade.

End of Act I

Act II

"Under a northern sky..."

Scene One

The set is the same as Act I. It is the following morning and as the lights come up we see the litter of the previous night everywhere: plates, glasses, bottles, the burned frying pan and so on.

*Enter **Moira**. She is scantily dressed in a dressing gown. She surveys the scene and groans.*

Moira: Fuckin toffs.

She gathers up the dishes and glasses and dumps them into the sink and begins to wash. Suddenly she stops as though she has had a change of mind, produces a cigarette packet from the pocket of her gown and lights up. She smokes for a minute and then begins to sing in a Country and Western accent

Moira: I was standin around in Jerusalem town one day
I was standin around in Jerusalem town one day
I was standin around in Jerusalem town one day-ay
an I said to myself "Hey, baby, I am the way"

Don't tell no body but I kissed Magdalene
Don't tell no body but I kissed Magdalene
Don't tell no body but I kissed Magdalene
right on the mouth
sayin it's okay Mary I am the way

She stubs out the cigarette and returns to the sink

Every son-a Gad has a little hard luck sometimes
Every son-a Gad has a little hard luck sometimes
Every son-a Gad has a little hard luck someti-himes
specially when he goes round sayin he's the way

Oh I am the way
yoodle lee hee hoo
I am the way

*She is so immersed in her song and her washing that she does not notice **Blacksmith** enter. He is dressed as before, as he is always dressed: ready for business.*

Blacksmith: Is everyone up?

Moira: (*turning in a fright*) Oh ya hoor, dinna do that!

Blacksmith: I'm sorry, I didn't mean to frighten you. I...

Moira: It's alright. I've got a terrible hangover.

Blacksmith: I'm just about to go out. Everyone else is asleep, I imagine?

Moira: Wrong there, mister. Everyone else is oot. they're all doon on the links. Looking for eggs or somethin.

Blacksmith: Ah yes, the plovers.

Moira: That's no what they call them. Shooits, or somethin? By the by, who the hell are you?

Blacksmith: (*offering a hand*) Sorry. I'm Brian Blacksmith. I'm lodging with Miss Swanson for a few weeks.

Moira: Then yer a brave man, Gungha Din.

Blacksmith: (*still with his hand out*) I'm sorry?

Moira: That ould dyke, she eats up most men for breakfast.

Blacksmith: As I say, it's only for a few weeks. The work should be over by then.

Moira: (*uninterestedly*) What work is it ye're doin, anyway?

Blacksmith: I'm surveying the whole area. It's quite a lengthy process.

Moira: It wouldnae take five minutes to survey this place. It's as flat as a pancake, surrounded by bogs, big cliffs an sea.

Blacksmith: Yes, but there's more to it than that. This coast has something I can't quite describe.

Moira: Well, if ye mean it's extremely borin I'll go along wi ye there.

Blacksmith: I rather think the opposite. Maybe it's just the sound of the sea and the way the land seems to rise up out of it and how it melds into the mountains beyond. And then there are the people. They seem to be made up of all three.

Moira: Good God, man, this is the North Pole! I wouldnae live here if ye paid me a million quid.

Blacksmith: Then you are a stranger to this coast?

Moira: Ay, an long may it continue. As long as I can keep Seoras away from that crazy dyke aunt o his.

Blacksmith: Miss Swanson seems like a regular farmer to me. Admittedly she has her ways…

Moira: Ways! Aye, she has her ways. Right hand doon the front o any stupid young lassie's pants. That's her way. I can recognise her type a mile off.

Blacksmith: You're being a bit unfair…

Moira: Ye're just lucky ye're no a woman. She only *hates* you lot.

> ***Blacksmith*** *ponders this for a moment, more in a state of shock than anything else. It is beyond him and he gives up on it.*

Blacksmith: What I've found in the short time I've been here is that the people seem to be in harmony with their environment. I've only come across this once before and that was in Africa. Quite remarkable.

Moira: Ye a fuckin hippy or somethin?

Blacksmith: I beg your pardon?

Moira: Well, excuse me, but I dinna ken too much aboot this neck o the woods right enough, but if Seoras is anythin tae go by the only harmony he seems tae hev is when his dick is in his hand. An if his daft sister is anythin tae go by then the women seem tae hev marbles rollin around loose upstairs. An as for the aunt, well weld my knickers on with a blow-torch!

Blacksmith: You seem to have a rather jaundiced view of the north.

Moira: No. I dinna think so. Mebbe it's ye that has things the wrong way roond. (*she goes over to the dresser and rummages in a cupboard*) Where is it? I saw a vodka bottle here earlier on. Ah, here it is. An the lemonade, magic! (*she goes to the table and pours herself a large drink*) Would you like one?

Blacksmith: Goodness gracious no!

Moira: Hell's teeth, man, it's a funeral! There's a stiff lyin through the wall. They're goin tae bury him later on wae all that moanin an chantin. The drink'll be flowin lek sheeps' piss. Get it while ye can! (*she drinks*)

Blacksmith: Still, no thank you. I have a morning's work to do yet.

Moira: Ahcourse. I was forgettin. (*she drinks*)

Blacksmith: Accuracy is of the utmost in this endeavour. And anyway, I try not to drink very much.

Moira: Very wise. (*she drinks*) Must be hard on ye, especially when ye're surrounded by such a bunch o pissheads like this lot. An dinna give me any spiel aboot their "character" or "culture" or whatever it was. I ken different. I used tae work in the West End Hotel in Edinburgh. All the hoochter choochters o the day would drink in there when they were in town. That's where I met Seoras. He was one o them. I saw them when they were drunk an I saw them when they were sober. A sorrier-lookin bunch o dickheads it was hard tae imagine.

She empties her glass and refills it.

Blacksmith: (*perplexed*) But you married Seoras, surely…

Moira: Ay, I married him. Look, he was good-lookin an he could hold his whisky. The rest o them were pug ugly, got gassed rapid an pissed in the rubber plants. An there were other reasons. (*she drinks*)

Blacksmith: (*moving over to the window*) Well, the rain seems to have stopped.

Moira: Ye dinnae hev tae ask. Ye're here tae survey the land, no the people.

Blacksmith: It's the people who will benefit from what we are doing. I wish I could make them believe it.

Moira: I dinna care what ye're doin. But ye'll never make them believe anythin. No this lot.

Blacksmith: On reflection, it's hardly surprising, considering their history. The poverty here, from what I can gather, was terrible and long-lasting. Scattering the population to the four corners of the world.

Moira: Oh God, ye're as bad as Seoras. Man, he goes on an on like a burst bagpipe aboot ruined crofts an sunken herrin boats. Ye'd think naebody else had been poor. They're so bloody smug aboot it. My mother was "cleared" frae Leith an we were stuck on the top story o a multi miles away oot on the edge o the toon. Nae shops, nae nothin. My faither buggered off years ago an we had tae make do however we could, an there was five o us. I've had tae do things for money, pal, that I'm far frae proud o. But that's another story. (*she drinks*)

Blacksmith: I'm sure. You know, it's the eradication of poverty that really is my ultimate aim. You see... eh... (*he waits for her to say her name; she doesn't*) ...we live in a finite world and if this society insists on going on as it is then it needs energy to meet its needs and to ensure its development. It is the providing of this energy which is the function of the modern scientist. What I am doing here is part of the process, part of the search.

Moira: My uncle Wullie was a miner at Bilston Glen. It was a brand new colliery wae years o life left in it. Still has but noo it's shut an Wullie's on the dole an taken tae the drink. An why no? At his age he'll never work again.

Blacksmith: But coal, all hydrocarbons, are finite, you see. Nuclear energy is infinite, at least in theory. Sometimes I think I'm in danger of going insane assuring people of its safety and practicality. But...

Moira: So why don't people believe ye?

Blacksmith: The same reason your uncle's colliery was closed: politics, or rather, politicians. The nuclear industry has been welded to the Ministry of Defence for too long and much to we scientists' disgust. We are in the business of creating the conditions for life to thrive, not to provide the means for its total destruction.

Moira: Ye sure ye dinna want a drink?

Blacksmith: Absolutely not. I must be going.

Moira: (*getting up rather unsteadily and going over to* **Blacksmith**) Ye ken, ye're no too different frae me.

Blacksmith: No?

Moira: I mean, neither o us wants tae be here. We're both strangers. We're both lost. We should stick thegither, eh? What d'ye say?

Blacksmith: I don't know what you mean.

> **Moira** *moves up very close to him and speaks the words huskily into his ear.*

Moira: Oh I think ye do, I think ye ken very weel. (*she strokes his tie*) Ye look like a lonely frustrated soul tae me.

Blacksmith: I'm perfectly content, I-I-assure you.

> **Moira** *undoes her dressing gown.*

Moira: Ye'll never ken, mister scientist, until ye try.

> **Blacksmith** *moves away from her as if he has been struck by a huge electric current. Enter* **Seoras**, **Shona**, **Henry** *and* **Marni**. *In one movement* **Moira** *does herself up and returns to the sink. The four are all fresh from the outdoors.* **Seoras** *goes over to* **Moira** *and caresses her gently.*

Seoras: Ye needna do that.

Moira: Don't worry. I ken my place.

Marni: Good til see the fryin pan's been washed. We've got a fair rake o eggs here.

Shona: (*to Blacksmith*) We shouldna really hev taken any, but there were literally hunners, so we just took one from each nest.

Blacksmith: I'm sure they can carry that.

Henry: Shona's very particular about the rights of animals. I don't think we've been introduced. I'm Henry. (*he extends his hand*)

Blacksmith: (*taking it eagerly*) I'm Brian Blacksmith. I'm...

Shona: Oh dinna tell us, wae know all aboot ye.

Blacksmith: Oh, I see. Well, I hope it's good.

Shona: It's utterly dreadful! Ye're a horrible man an ye want til poison the planet!

Blacksmith: Ah, I see. The usual.

Marni: Pay nae heed til her, Doctor. Her head's way in the clouds. (*to Moira, looking at the vodka glass and taking the frying pan from the sink*) Good til see ye're sober.

Moira: What d'ye ken aboot bein sober, anyway?

Seoras: Just fry the eggs, Marni. I'm starvin!

Blacksmith: (*to Shona as she unpacks the eggs*) Do I look like a work of evil to you then? Do I look like a poisoner?

Shona: It's hard til tell. They all wear suits these days.

Blacksmith: "They"? Who's "they"?

Shona: Oh, ye know, the usual: liars, thieves, con men, dumpers.

Henry: But Doctor Blacksmith is a nuclear physicist, Shona. To him his motives are as pure as day. Is that not so, Doctor?

Blacksmith: Quite so.

Shona: Ye're ower easily led, Henry. Behind that facade o respectability an normality there lurks a seethin an schemin psychopath. Doctor Death is just bidin his time!

> *Henry laughs*

Blacksmith: I must say, this is just too much. You've only just met me! (*he tries to laugh too, but it comes out forced*)

Shona: Doctor Death is weel kent here.

Marni: Shona, do somethin useful an go an get the bacon. Ye'll be needin a spot o breakfast yersel, Doctor Dea... eh, I mean, Doctor.

Blacksmith: Uh, no thank you. I have to be going.

Marni: Nonsense. Ye hev til eat.

Shona: (*as she exits*) Bury it under the hooses o Parliament if it's so safe!

Blacksmith: (*to Henry*) Well, that game turned rather sour.

Henry: Shona's beliefs are deeply felt.

> *Moira crosses over to the Raeburn where Marni has begun cooking.*

Seoras: (*from the sink*) The only trouble is she doesna know what the hell she's talkin aboot. As usual.

Henry: She's entitled to speak her mind.

Seoras: She's my sister an lek me she doesna hev a mind. Ah, what a glorious smell!

Moira: You'll be happier when yer stomach's full, Seoras. Another desire satisfied.

Marni: Well there's eggs here aplenty. Enough til feed a regiment. Ye sure ye'll no hev just a tastie, Doctor? Ye'll no hev hed the shochad eggs afore?

Blacksmith: You're quite right there.

Seoras: They're as sweet as the mornin air. Ye can taste the springtime in them.

Henry: You'll be missing a rare treat, Doctor.

Marni: Go on, man, hang the surveyin for half an hoor.

Blacksmith: Oh, alright then. But I can't stay long.

Marni: Good man. Seoras, go set the table an stop standin there lek a sick stirk.

Henry: I'll get the plates.

Moira: Why don't ye waggle yer tits as well, boys?

Seoras: Just shut up, Moira.

> *The two men busy themselves with their tasks, as does* **Moira**.
> **Blacksmith** *moves over to* **Marni**.

Blacksmith: Ah, they really do smell delicious.

Marni: Best part o this time o year.

Blacksmith: This coastland is spectacular in the springtime. We're covering the mouth of the strath this morning so I'll miss the sound of the sea. But then there's the gorse. It's so beautiful. It smells like coconuts.

Marni: Whins!

Blacksmith: I'm sorry?

Marni: Whins, Doctor, they're cried whins, no gorse.

Henry: Very English, "gorse".

Blacksmith: Well, I am English.

> *Enter* **Shona** *with the bacon*

Shona: Is this Billy Bannerman's best? (*she moves over to* **Marni**)

Marni: The very same. Slaughtered the sou mysel.

Seoras: God, ye're a pagan, Auntie Marni.

Marni: Deil the fear o it, boy. Billag's been rearin saddlebacks for ower thirty year but he still canna bring hissel til kill them.

Blacksmith: How do you do it? The butchering, I mean?

Marni: Easy. Ye just sit ahint their head. Grab their snout wae yer left han, an slit their gizzard wae yer richt. It's ower in a twinkle. The peeg knows naethin aboot it.

Seoras: D'ye still catch the blood in a basin?

Marni: Of course. The best black puddin there is comes frae the peegie.

Henry: I thought it was illegal to slaughter animals on the farm.

Scoras: (*to Henry*) Marni's aye had scant regard for any laws savin her own.

Marni: If I spent muckle time worryin aboot feel daft laws tellin me what I could an couldna do I'd get no bloody fermin done at all. Here now, plates up!

> *Henry moves over to her with a pile of plates and Marni dishes up the eggs. She proceeds to cook the bacon. Shona distributes the plates onto their places.*

Shona: Breakfast everyone!

> *She goes to a cupboard and produces a loaf of bread. They all sit except for Marni.*

Marni: Man, ye canna beat the smell o fresh grunter!

Scoras: God bless Beelag's sou.

Shona: Is that the Grace?

Scoras: Why no? I lek peegs.

Shona: That's because ye are one.

Scoras: Eat yer eggies, snouty.

Henry: The sky went pure blue after it stopped rainin. An the air. It was so amazingly pure.

Marni: Ay, it was grand. The wind was an easterly comin off the sea. Keeps everythin clean.

Moira: I'm glad somethin does.

Marni: Somethin botherin ye, my lassie? Spit it oot if there is.

Moira: It's glued tae the back o my throat, unfortunately.

Marni: Then it's a doctor ye're needin.

Moira: Doctors are no bloody use tae anybody.

Shona: D'ye hear what she's sayin aboot ye, Doctor Death?

Blacksmith: (*ignoring her epithet*) Medicine is not my field, I'm afraid. Now, if it were a nuclear particle, that would be a different proposition.

Marni: Ye say that now!

Shona: But we're all particles!

Scoras: Ay, an ye've got a few loose.

Shona: But we are! We're all made up o an infinite amount o them. Is that no right, Doctor Death?

Marni: Shona, will ye keep a civil tongue in yer head. The mannie's name is Blacksmith.

Blacksmith: (*to Marni*) That's alright. I enjoy a joke too. (*to Shona*) Indeed we are made up of particles, but not, I'm afraid, an infinite number. They could all be counted, or at least estimated, if we had a mind to.

Scoras: Seems pretty pointless til me til know exactly how many nuclear particles ye're made o.

Blacksmith: Mathematics can save you the trouble. After all it is the language of the universe.

*Marni moves across to **Blacksmith** with the frying pan and dishes him out some rashers.*

Marni: An here' s the language o the stomach: grunter, fried an singin.

Blacksmith: Thank you. This is decidedly delicious.

Seoras: (*softly to **Moira***) Moira, ye've hardly touched yer eggs.

Moira: I'm no hungry. Ye can hev them.

Seoras: Darlin, ye must eat.

Moira: I've told ye. I'm no hungry. Take them.

Seoras: Ye sure?

Moira: For fuck's sake, ay!

Seoras scoops her eggs onto his plate.

Shona: Peeg!

Seoras: I telt ye, I lek peegs.

Marni goes round the table and dishes out some rashers to everyone. Then she puts on the kettle.

Henry: Come an have somethin yerself, Marni, you must be hungry, are you no?

Marni: I hed somethin when ye lot were still snorin. I hed til go oot an check on the lambs. A cuppa tea an a bap'll do me.

Shona: I love the way the shochads dive on ye. Peeeooooohwit! It's so dramatic an yet quite frightenin at the same time. It's queer, cos ye know they're never goin til hit ye.

Seoras: I widna be so sure.

Marni: I've never heard tell o it, I must say.

Shona: Ye're just a beeg baby, Seoras. Ye're still frichtened o the shochads. Same as wheen ye were a peedie loon.

Seoras: I seem til remember it wis ye who wis the frichtened one. But dinna underestimate the shochad. He's a bloody dangerous bird if he's a mind.

Shona: Oh, my poor lambie.

Henry: They're protecting their nests. They've every right to be aggressive.

Marni: If we were more lek the shochad on that score things might be different here.

Everybody chooses to ignore that remark.

Shona: I'd forgotten how beautiful the links are on a spring mornin, wae the surf crashin on the shore, the bleatin o the lambs an the cry o the birds.

Seoras: Peeeeooooohwhit!

Shona: Peeeeooooohwhit! They used til hev so many names. Lapwing, Plover, Peewit. We used til know them all.

Marni: A shochad's a shochad. I dinna see what all the fuss is aboot.

Shona: Dinna tell me it doesna get intil ye too, Auntie Marni? If no, why wid ye hev stayed here all these years?

Marni: My, where else wid ye hev me go?

Henry: (*to **Shona***) Marni's here like the land itself.

Marni: Ay, an I'm no movin if I can help it. The only way they'll get me oot o here is feet first.

There is a silence

Shona: Faither wid hev loved this mornin. He loved the shochads an all the other birds an floors on the links. He loved the springtime an the lambin. He loved everythin. (*she bursts into tears*)

Henry: (*putting his arms around her*) Come here, my love, it's alright, cry all you want.

Marni: He loved everythin save for hard work.

Seoras: Marni, that's enough! It's his funeral the day.

Marni: I'm sayin nothin I didna say til his face. I'm no hypocrite!

Seoras: Weel then, there's no need til repeat it at breakfast!

Marni: Ay, ye're right, loon. I'm sorry.

Seoras: (*laughing*) Did ye hear that, Shona? Auntie Marni said she was sorry! Hoist up the flags! (*he rises from the table and crosses to **Marni***) C'mere ye ould gimmer an I'll gie ye a bit dance.

*He pulls **Marni** from her chair and grabs her by the middle. She struggles.*

Marni: Ye'll do no such thing! An less o the ould gimmer frae ye, or it's the back o my han ye'll be gettin.

Seoras: Ach, wheesht wumman. Come on!

*He forces her into a rough waltz and despite herself **Marni** laughs and relaxes.*

Marni: It's a long time since these ould legs danced.

Seoras: There ye go. Just lek the ould hervest ceilidhs.

Shona: (*recovering slightly*) Watch he doesna stand on yer toes, Auntie Marni. He's such a goat.

Seoras: Away! Auntie Marni is transported wae the sheer poetry o the dance ontil a higher plane o consciousness.

***Marni** breaks free*

Marni: I am no such thing! The very thocht.

Seoras: I was forgettin, the only plane ye've been transported til was the hospital plane til Inverness when that coo kicked ye in the knee.

Marni: Ye cheeky monkey! C'mere til I gie ye a wallop! On second thochts, make the tea. I'm no just feelin great. (*she sits down*)

Shona: (*getting up and going over to her*) Are ye alright, Auntie Marni?

Marni: Ay, I'm fine. I just need a bit seat.

Shona: (*to **Seoras***) Ye great galoot! Ye shouldna be throwin yer auntie aboot lek thon!

Marni: Lassie, I'm no a china doll. I'll be alricht. I need a wee rest, that's all there is til it.

***Marni** rubs the back of her neck*

Moira: Have ye got a pain in the neck? (*she looks over at **Seoras***) I'm no surprised.

Marni: For yer information it's rheumatics, so ye dinna hev til worry that ye're causin me any pain.

Moira: I wasna.

Seoras: Moira, come over here an geez a hand wae the tea. The kettle's boilin.

Moira: (*mimicking Shona as she moves to him*) My poor wee lambie, is it all too much for ye?

Henry: How many lambs have ye got so far, Marni?

Marni: It's hard til tell. There's aboot a hunner ewes til go. I'll tell ye then.

Blacksmith: They are fine healthy-looking creatures anyway. There must be over four hundred on the hill at a rough estimate.

Marni: There ye go, Henry, the doctor knows more aboot it than mysel.

Blacksmith: It's the surveying, I'm afraid. The truth is that it really does get jolly boring at times. If it wasn't for this landscape I think I'd go mad. So one surveys other things.

Seoras: So ye count sheep? I dinna believe it!

Blacksmith: Sheep, deer, people, houses.

Seoras: Weel, hev ye counted how many are empty, doctor?

Blacksmith: I have noticed a significant number, I will admit.

Seoras: Oh, ye will admit it will ye? An d'ye ever wonder why they're empty?

Blacksmith: I'm not stupid. I know that they are mostly holiday homes.

Seoras: An did ye survey the fact that there's a housin shortage the length o this coat as weel?

Blacksmith: I am aware of it. I talk to the men.

Seoras: The men? Is this the men ye recruited in Wick? All sixty o them in thirty minutes flat for one fifty an hoor? Dinna turn up one mornin an that's ye sacked? Plenty more where they came frae? Eh, doctor?

Blacksmith: I don't make the terms of engagement. That is the business of the Authority.

Seoras: I dinna lek the business o yer bloody Authority!

Marni: Seoras, behave yersel, boy! The doctor's only doin his job.

Blacksmith: Which I must get to. (*he rises*) Thank you very much for a delicious breakfast.

Marni: Ye're welcome.

Blacksmith: (*to Marni*) If you want the doctor I can easily send to Bunillidh for him.

Seoras: We hev the phone!

Marni: (*to Blacksmith*) No thanks, loon, I'll be fine.

Blacksmith: Then I bid you all a good morning.

   Blacksmith exits

Seoras: (*to Marni*) What's he doin under this roof?

Marni: Payin his keep. Whit else?

Shona: Seoras, why d'ye hev til be so aggressive?

Seoras: (*turning*) I thocht ye'd be supporting me, at least?

Shona: I do, but…

Seoras: But what?

Moira: (*to Shona*) Yer self-righteousness makes me sick, that's what ye want tae say, isn't it?

Shona: No.

Marni: The man's no personally responsible for the evils o the world, Seoras.

Seoras: I know, I know, "he wis only doin his job". There were guys sayin that at Dachau.

- **Henry:** Quite so, but you don't want to be like Mhairi Mhor, Seoras, cursin the factor an forgettin the Duke.

Seoras: Bonglies, God save us frae bonglies!

Moira: An God save us frae wimps who want tae change the world by havin everythin stay the same.

Henry: Very profound, Moira.

> *Moira mumbles something unintelligible under her breath*

Marni: (*standing up*) Weel, if ye're all finished we can clear the table.

> *Marni starts to clear the table. Shona goes over to the Raeburn.*

Shona: Tea everybody?

Moira: (*getting up*) Uh, God, I'm gonnae be sick!

> *She grabs her vodka glass and exits.*

Seoras: Moira!

> *He looks sheepish for a moment, then dashes off after her*

Shona: Poor Seoras.

Marni: More fool him for marryin the thing.

Henry: We shouldn't criticise what folk feel, because it's impossible to know.

Shona: Is it, I wonder?

Henry: I think so.

> *She moves over to him and cradles his head*

Shona: Oh Henry, that's such a terribly masculine thing til say.

Henry: Is it?

Marni: God knows nor cares! Where's my bloody tea?

Shona: (*springing back to the Raeburn*) Sorry, Auntie Marni.

> *Shona pours the tea. Marni drinks hers eagerly and smacks her lips.*

Marni: Aah, that's more lek the thing. (*pause*) Weel, looks lek he's gettin a fine day for his funeral, if it holds. Been known til snow at this time o year, but he wis aye lucky lek that.

Henry: There'll be a big turnout, I imagine.

Marni: Ay, there will that. All the farmers frae along the coast, an up the strath, an more.

Shona: They'll be honourin the Swanson dead. Hector Swanson was one o them. They'll be wantin til pay their respects.

Marni: An they'll all be wantin a dram. An fed, if I'm no mistaken.

Shona: The drink's easy. But how are we goin til feed them?

Marni: Ach, there's a side o beef hingin in the scullery. We'll roast that an that'll do em.

Shona: Good.

Marni: The hoose'll be fill o all their bitches, cluckin aboot the place lek noisy hens.

Shona: They mean weel, Marni, an ye hev til let tradition hev its way.

Marni: Tradition, my hips. All they want til do is clash an blether. Ye can feel the skin bein stripped off ye. Weel they're no comin through here! This kitchen's oota bounds!

Shona: Auntie Marni!

Henry: I've never been to a Grey Coast funeral before.

Marni: (*snappily*) Oh my, then this'll be an edjication fir ye!

Shona: I still canna believe that he's deid. I still expect him til walk in here at any minute.

Henry: We're all still in a state of shock, Shona. Soon it'll be over, then we'll have to deal with our grief.

Marni: Why should we grieve fir the deid? Blubbering never brocht anybody back.

Henry: My God, have you no heart in you? Don't you feel anythin?

Marni: Ay, I feel irritated that hae hed til go afore the lambin wis finished. This whole business is gettin me doon. I'll be gled when tomorrow comes an life can get back til normal.

Henry: I've never met anybody so hard.

Marni: Then ye hevna lived, boy. But that doesna surprise me. Here the deid just get in the way. They follow ye lek a plough does a tractor. The deid should bide in the kirkyard where we put em. I swear there's more deid folk than living souls on the go the day.

Shona: But they're no all cried Swanson.

Marni: More's the pity!

Henry: Shona, I'm going up to lie down for a bit. Are you coming?

Shona: In a minute. I'll just tidy up here a little bittie first.

Henry: Very good.

He stares at **Marni** *coldly for a second, then exits.*

Shona: Auntie Marni, ye shouldna say things lek that in front o Henry. He thinks ye mean them. Hae doesna understan.

Marni: Weel, hae should, an so should ye. I meant every word.

Shona: Marni, how could ye?

Marni: Ach, it's alricht for the lek o ye, Shona, ye come back home every now an again an ye get all dewy-eyed aboot the place. It's understandable. Ye mind the fine things when ye were a bairn. The bonny spring-times an the long simmer dim. But ye forget the long black winter nichts that stretch for months until a body's fair demented frae it. The continual blast o the gale an storm that goes on until ye feel ye're hingin ontil this coast by yer very fingers. Ye see, Shona, ye live in yer heid. Ye dinna live here.

Shona: Ye really hate us, Seoras an me, don't ye?

Marni: Hate ye? Naa, I dinna hate ye. It's just… ach I dinna know, lassie, the years speed by ye an sometimes a body feels alone. Ever since yer mither died there's been no one, I a… ach!

> *Marni sags visibly. Shona goes over to her and holds her close. It's as if Marni is beginning to relax for the first time in years. Her eyes fill with the tears of that tension and they flood down her cheeks.*

Shona: There, Auntie Marni, it's okay. It's fine.

Marni: Oh I loved her, Shona. She was the most beautiful soul who ever walked the earth.

Shona: I know.

Marni: Helen wis lek those summer nichts ye mind. We'd walk the links an then up the strath til the broch. We'd sit an yarn their fir hoors, an then back here til the ferm. Helen kept me sane. But whan we got back we'd hev til be quate for if he saw us thegither lek thon he'd glower an scowl. Black jealous hae wis.

Shona: It wis only natural.

Marni: Ay, I s'pose so. I was jealous when I saw her wae him. Oh, Shona, Shona, it's all so fuckin complicated.

Shona: No it's no. Ye loved her. It's quite simple. Really.

Marni: Ay, but no here, no then. Their eyes were always on us. Every move noted. Every thocht seen.

Shona: Ye did naethin wrong. My mither must've needed love too. I know what went on. I heard them arguin an fightin. Seoras knows too, but he never says anythin.

Marni: Than hae's wise. I've said ower muckle already.

Shona: Naa, Auntie Marni, ye're all I've got left here on this coast. Both Seoras an mysel, weel, he'll never say it, but we love ye very much.

Marni: Ye're so lek her, d'ye ken that?

Shona: So ye say. I'm gled.

Marni: Me too. (*she kisses Shona gently on the cheek, then breaks free*) Noo, the deid coo. We'd better slam her in the oven the abernow or all they fermer mannies'll be girnin from here til Christmas. An we'd better check we've enough whisky. Their beeg reid faces'll be needin an extra glow the day. C'mon now, my lambie, yer ould auntie's needin a han.

> *Exit Marni and Shona, hand in hand.*

Scene Two

It is afternoon. The kitchen is set out for a reception. A roast sits carved on the table. There are bottles, glasses, plates and cutlery set out on the dresser in organised chaos. Despite this everything looks neat and prepared. there is the sound, from offstage, of muffled conversation from many souls in another room.

Enter **Moira**, *obviously the worse for drink, but holding it well. She goes over to the dresser and pours herself a generous measure of vodka which she tops up with lemonade. she sinks down into a chair and lights a cigarette.*

Enter **Seoras**. *He looks drawn and anxious.*

Seoras: There ye are.

Moira: I'm sorry, Seoras, but I couldnae stand it any more. It's like bein in a time machine. They go back an back intae the past. An anyway, that big ugly red bastard Bannerman put his hand on my arse.

Seoras: He did no.

Moira: Well mebbe no. But he was goin tae.

Seoras: (*kneeling down before her*) Look, I know ye're no happy here, but we hev til stay a few days more, an then after that we can go home.

Moira: Home? Where the hell's that?

Seoras: Edinburgh.

Moira: My feet! Ye're home the now, Seoras, an ye'll never leave this fuckin place. I kent it as soon as ye telt me we were tae come here.

Seoras: No. Home is wherever you are. I love ye, Moira.

Moira: Oh God! (*she rises suddenly and moves over to the window*) Just look at the fuckin weather. It's chuckin it doon.

Seoras: (*coming up behind her*) Seasonal, I'm afraid. It changes quickly. Just lek ye.

Moira: (*turning to face him*) Ye've absolutely nae idea who the hell I am, hev ye? I dinna change, Seoras, I just decline. Has yer auntie no telt ye aboot my kind, I bet she has.

Seoras: Stop this. I love ye.

Moira: (*moving away*) Stop sayin ye love me, will ye?

Seoras: Why? What's wrong?

Moira: What's wrong? Christ, I dinna ken. What's no wrong?

Seoras: Look, what more can I give ye that'll make ye happy? Ye've got a hoose, me, security. I mean...

Moira: I dinna ken what I want. That's the problem. All my life I've been lookin, lookin, lookin, an for what? I havena a fuckin clue. An yet I ken when I see it I'll be happy.

Seoras: (*holding her*) Ach, Moira, I want ye til be happy. I really do. I'll do anything. I married ye because I thocht that wid make ye happy.

Moira: But has it made ye happy? I dinnae think so. Look, I'm no good for ye, canna ye see it. Ye need one o they grey coast lassies that are in kitchens lek this from north tae south. All hens an earth an honest-

tae-Christ baking. Ye dinna really want me. I'm none o they things.
(*she drinks*)

Seoras: Dinna drink lek that, Moira. It only depresses ye.

Moira: That's right, Seoras, I'm depressed. Poor Moira. Doesnae ken
whit she wants, doesnae appreciate what she's got. Poor Moira.

Seoras: Then what am I s'posed til do for ye then? How can I help ye?

Moira: Fuckin well leave me alone.

Seoras: But I'm goin offshore in a couple o weeks. Ye can be on yer
own then.

Moira: No. Never in that flat. Ye're everywhere in it. Everythin is yers.
The wallpaper, the furniture, the carpets, everythin.

Seoras: Then buy a new flat.

Moira: No Seoras, it's no that easy. Ye canna buy yer way oot o trouble.
Yer Swanson money's nae use tae ye here, I'm afraid.

Seoras: (*sitting down*) Do what ye want then.

Moira: (*moving over to him and running her fingers through his hair*)
Cannae ye see how hard that is for me? At the moment I canna see
straight, I cannae think right. I've got tae find oot what's wrong wae
me. I've got tae admit a few things tae mysel. Ye dinnae want me
endin up like yer mother.

Seoras: (*standing up*) What d'ye mean?! Dinna ye dare talk aboot her!

Moira: Why? Because I havenae got the right? Because I'm no a
Swanson? Weel, ye're right, I'll never be a Swanson! I may hev yer
name on a marriage certificate, but I'll never be yers!

Seoras: Ye just dinna know how fortunate ye are! Ye should... ye
should... Ach!

Moira: What?

Seoras: Nothin. Forget it.

Moira: (*taunting*) C'mon, what? That I should be grateful? Is that it, eh?
Eh? Weel, I'll show ye how fuckin grateful I am!

> *She takes off her wedding ring and throws it at him. There is a*
> *silence.* **Moira** *drinks from her glass. Suddenly she looks frightened.*

Moira: Seoras, I...

> *Enter* **Struan Cheyne**, *as merry as a Sheriff.*

Cheyne: Ah, there you are, my boy. I haven't had a chance to have a
word with the North Sea Tiger since he's come home to his native lair.

Moira: I'm goin tae be sick.

> *She exits*

Cheyne: Spritely thing. Something I said?

Seoras: Pay no heed, Struan, all this business has upset her. (*he shakes
Cheyne's hand*) How are ye doin? Brought back the black cap yet?

Cheyne: (*chuckling*) No, not yet. I'll miss your father, Seoras. Hector
was a good friend.

Seoras: Ay, weel, what can ye say? We all knew it was comin, but it's
still a shock.

Cheyne: You know, it's a pity your father wasn't a solicitor. Man, they live forever.

Seoras: (*laughing*) Weel, ye should know, Struan. A dram?

Cheyne: Ay, why not? A brandy if you've got it. That aunt of yours has fairly thirled me off the whisky.

Seoras: (*pouring*) Ach weel, progress. (*he hands **Cheyne** the drink*)

Cheyne: Well, here's to my friend and your father, Hector Swanson. One of the best men on this coast. May he rest in peace.

Seoras: Amen til that. (*they drink*)

Cheyne: I've never seen so many black ties and bonnets in a long time. The ewes can go and lamb themselves the day. Even Sinclair the minister made sense.

Seoras: Ay, I think he wis shocked intil lucidity by the sheer numbers.

Cheyne: So how's the oil industry treating you, Seoras? They tell me you're a driller now, what ever that may mean or be?

Seoras: Ay, I'm a driller, newly promoted last month. An it means just what it means – I drill for oil.

Cheyne: No chance of you drilling in my back park is there? A chap could use the lolly.

Seoras: Man, they're producin off the coast here. Is that no enough for ye?

Cheyne: (*snorting*) That's as maybe, Seoras, but it never seems to reach Bunillidh. D'you know Jim Henderson's boy works on one of those two platforms – what do they call the confounded things again?

Seoras: The Beatrice Alpha an Brava.

Cheyne: That's right, the Beatrice. Well he has to go all the way to Aberdeen to get on it!

Seoras: It is daft, I'll admit, but that's the way o it. My rig's currently west o Shetland an we fly over here both on the way up an doon. Can even see the ferm here when the weather's good.

Cheyne: Never feel like bailing out?

Seoras: Without a parachute? Naa, Struan, I think I'll leave that til the sheriffs an ministers o this world. Them that disna need them. (*pause*) Anyway, I reckon I baled out years ago.

Cheyne: But now you're head of the Swanson family. Being the first named male in the estate this farm is yours. That's after Marni goes, mind you. And I think you might have to wait a while for that.

Seoras: An what o Shona? It's hers too?

Cheyne: Yes, but there will be three shares and two of you. D'you see what I mean?

Seoras: I know fine what ye mean.

Cheyne: This is good land, Seoras, some o the best on the coast. A man could do well here.

Seoras: An ye mean a wumman couldna?

Cheyne: It's just that your aunt – well, she's gone about things in a rather weird and wasteful fashion of late.

Seoras: What d'ye mean?

Cheyne: Well, you see that big new barn she's built at the back of the steading – the old steading having mysteriously burned down. Well, that barn contains the biggest grain blow-dryer in the Highlands. She's turned all the arable ground over to barley which she grows under license from the EC. And she contracts in other farmers' grain to make her dryer pay.

Seoras: Weel, what's wrong wae that?

Cheyne: Simple economics, dear boy. There is a mountain of grain in the storehouses of Europe as high as the Alps. The price of barley has fallen through the floor. The banks are knocking hard at your good aunt's door, curse them! They lend you an umbrella when it's a sunny day and ask for it back when it's raining.

Seoras: So what's she goin til do?

Cheyne: What else can she do? Sell.

Seoras: Marni Swanson sell Bunillidh Mains! Are ye mad? They'd hev til kill her first!

Cheyne: Believe me, she agrees with you. But they're killing her now. Or rather, she's killing herself. No amount of Swanson pride and stubbornness will get her out of this one. Unless... (*pause*)

Seoras: Unless what? (*pause*) Now let me just guess.

Cheyne: But it would make perfect sense. You could convince her to hand over the reins to you. Pretty it up any way you like, but do it you must. Seoras, if you were to take over the farm the banks could be convinced to hold off. A new broom, all that sort of thing. You could cut back on your acreage of grain – the price is bound to rise in a year or so. Bring back cattle. Grow more silage, neeps, that sort of thing. Maybe sell off your links land. You don't really need it – and get rid of these damn' sheep. They strip the hills like maggots anyway. That at least will give you some working capital.

Seoras: Hey, hey, hold on there, Sheriff! Ye're miles ahead o me.

Cheyne: Seoras, this old grey coast of ours is dying. If this farm goes how long before the next one and the next one? Our native stock is being thinned already. Foreigners are buying up holdings here like nobody's business. How soon before there's nothing but tourists and museums?

Seoras: I know! I know! I know! (*pause*) But the decision has been made for me already.

Cheyne: How come? I don't understand.

Seoras: When the company asked me til be a driller they were askin all sorts o ither questions too. Lek this coastland the oil industry doesna encourage ye til stay still. They were sayin til me: promotion or cheerio? I took promotion an all that goes wae it. Once ye're a driller, Struan, ye canna pussyfoot around anymore. Guys' lives are at stake. There's no room for anythin else.

Cheyne: Not even this farm, your family name?

Seoras: Struan, they kent fine what they were askin! They let ye make the decision. They make ye choose. They're smart lek that. Very smart.

Cheyne: You make it sound like you've sold your soul.

Seoras: Weel, mebbe I hev.

Cheyne: Oh God, how very Scottish! I think I need another drink.

He pours himself a brandy. **Cheyne** *narrows his brows as if he has suddenly developed a sore head. He walks over to the window and stares out, his eyes burning everything in their sight.*

Cheyne: Seoras, I think you're not looking at this the right way. How long will the oil last? Another fifteen years? Maybe more, maybe less. What are you going to do then? Where will you be?

Seoras: Oh I dinna think I'll be in the North Sea or anywhere near it by then. No, Struan, I plan til see a bit o the world an in this job I can.

Cheyne: (*trying not to lose his temper*) But the oil will run out everywhere eventually.

Seoras: I hardly think I need worry aboot that.

Cheyne *turns on his heel, his face red and his eyes focused on* **Seoras** *like a beacon.*

Cheyne: And what will you be on your drilling rig then, Seoras, what promotions will you have attained then? An exploiter? An appropriator? A mercenary stealing a resource from a local people who need its benefits more than your American paymasters? A good job that, Seoras, eh? A fine job that!

Seoras: (*aggrieved*) Ye've got a bloody cheek til lecture me on morality, Struan Cheyne! My God, ye've bent the rules all yer life!

Cheyne: Which is why I can see clearly what's going on. What actual benefits have those oil fields out there ever brought to this land or its people? We must be unique in being so rich and so poor at the same time! If people such as yourself don' stay on the land and work it when they have the chance then what good is our history, what good is our future? What good is anything?

Seoras: Weel, for one thing, I dinna need ye til tell me aboot it. Landed gentry are always tellin poor folk what til do. That's a lesson o history ye probably dinna lek. We came here wae naethin, an if this land that ye get so worked up aboot is so great then it's because o people lek us who forced it by muscle an sweat til give them what they needed. I canna thole this romantic nonsense aboot the mystical nature o the soil! It's all a sham frae people who dinna know better. When I look at these parks I see fields o sea wrack, cattle shite an nitrogen.

Cheyne: So you're going to give them up just like that? You're going to turn your back on those generations of effort?

Seoras: I dinna know what I'm goin til do, but I never turn my back on anythin!

Cheyne: Weel, I hope so, Seoras, I hope so. You see, old boy, I think your aunt will sell.

Seoras: Really?

Cheyne: I can't see any other way out of it for her. She's tried various things before. She even burned down the old steading. It was only because of myself and a few others that she got the insurance and didn't get the jail instead.

Seoras: Are ye serious?

Cheyne: Absolutely, old chap. Never underestimate your aunt. She's as hard as nails and fly with it. She'll try to sell this place over your head, knowing full well that if you disputed the sale and took her to court, she'd lose, only having the one full share. She's banking on the fact that neither you or Shona would allow the Swanson name to be dragged through the mud.

Seoras: I dinna believe ye.

Cheyne: Then go look at the charred remains of the old steading. I tell you this: if it wasn't for the wind changing direction when it did that night we would not have a kitchen to talk in. She was lucky then. But no more.

Seoras: (*slightly stunned*) I know Auntie Marni's a bittie off the wall, but I didna think that she'd... that she could've...

Cheyne: She knows there's only one way out for her.

Seoras: But if she sells, I mean, where'll she go?

Cheyne: Who knows? Anywhere, except on this coast. She won't stay here. She can't. Not without land to work. My reckoning is that she'll go south to die.

Seoras: Ye're being ower dramatic! I've never heard so much dirt!

Cheyne: My dear boy, I've told you – never underestimate your aunt!

Seoras: Believe me, I dinna, but...

Cheyne: But nothing. She's ruthless and will do anything to get what she wants.

Seoras: Just what the hell *does* she want, exactly?

Cheyne: She wants to retain her power, and to do that she has to retain her money. The rest will follow.

Seoras: Ye mean she wants what's due til Shona an mysel?

Cheyne: Exactly, an only you an Shona can stop her.

Seoras: You make her sound lek a maniac!

Cheyne: Seoras, I have known your aunt for over forty years.

Seoras: Ach, I dunno. I'll hev til talk til Shona aboot it. That's if she'll listen. She refuses til see the bad side o any Swanson, especially her beloved aunt.

> *Enter* **Shona**. **Seoras** *slumps in a chair and nurses his drink.*

Cheyne: (*effusively*) My dear girl, at long last I have you all to myself!

> *He grabs her and kisses her on her forehead.*

Shona: Struan, I saw ye earlier, mind?

Cheyne: Oh I know, I know, but we were surrounded by the talking bunnets. And that doesn't count.

Shona: (*freeing herself*) Weel, they're the drinkin bunnets now. Seoras, I'm worried about Marni. She's as fill as a wilk.

Seoras: (*moodily*) Whit's new?

Shona: But it's no the same as usual. There's somethin manic aboot her the now.

Cheyne: Your aunt is going through a tricky time of it at the moment, Shona, the pressure has to show itself somehow.

Shona: She's no the only one! I just buried ma faither ower an hoor ago!

Cheyne: (*putting his arm around her*) I know, my dear, I know.

Seoras: Shona, we hev til talk.

Shona: Ay, whit aboot exactly?

Seoras: Ach, everything.

> *Enter* **Marni** *followed by* **Henry** *with a worried look on his face*

Marni: (*drunkenly*) Whaddye mean by desertin yer ould auntie, the pair o ye?

Shona: We didna desert ye, Auntie Marni, ye're surrounded by folk.

Marni: (*pouring herself a drink*) No by my ain blood. No now, anyway.

Cheyne: Must you be so morbid? Hector's gone and God bless him in his rest. But you, you hardly ever spoke to him in years.

Marni: There's more ways til say what ye mean than by usin words. That's something ye book-learned lounge-lawyers'll never know.

Seoras: Marni, this is neither the time nor the place for such talk.

Marni: (*to* **Seoras**) I'll grieve for yer mither, an long will I do it. But never for yer faither!

Shona: (*close to tears*) How can ye speak lek this?

Marni: Cause he wanted til take it away frae me, an I widna let em. I saw through his schemes. I see through all yer schemes!

Henry: What schemes are these, exactly?

Marni: (*snappily*) Keep yer neb oot o it, boy. Ye dinna belong.

Shona: Auntie Marni!

Henry: It's okay, Shona, it's okay.

Marni: Weel, ye're gettin nothin, none o ye! Ye've done nothin, an ye're gettin nothin!

Cheyne: I would watch what you say, old girl, this kind of discussion about such matters is far from advisable.

Marni: Struan, shuddup! I'm seek o yer sanctimonious opinions an yer beeg fat face. Why dinna ye clear off an leave us alone?!

Cheyne: (*angrily*) If it were not for the presence of Hector's fine children I would do so, but not before I'd cut out your tongue! But after I leave today, Miss (*he hisses the word*) Swanson, I shall not return! You can stew in your own juice this time. God alone knows you've had it coming to you!

> **Seoras** *tries to calm* **Cheyne** *as* **Marni** *makes child-like mimicking faces from across the table.*

Seoras: Hang fire, Struan bouyag, calm doon. She's truly flipped this time.

Cheyne: (*calming down*) Quite right, old chap, quite right. All the same, I think I'd better be going.

Shona: (*grabbing hold of his arm*) No! Dinna go, Struan, no yet.

Henry: Ay, Struan, stay a while yet. We may have need of ye before the night is out.

Marni: (*snarling*) So ye're all turnin on me now, eh? Weel, I dinna need any o ye!

Shona: (*trying to approach her*) Auntie Marni, for goodness' sake clam doon. This is ma faither's funeral. Yer brither.

Marni: Ma brither? (*she grunts out a laugh*) He's no brither o mine. Tried til kill me. No word o a lie.

Seoras: Ye're haverin, Marni.

Marni: (*staring Seoras in the face*) I'm tellin ye. When I wis under the scaffoldin. We were tryin til rebuild the far steadin wall. He waited until my back wis turned an dropped a nine inch block ontil the back o my heid. What ye make o that, Seoras?

Cheyne: Hector did no such thing. You should be ashamed of yourself.

Marni: (*to Cheyne*) His aim wisna as good as he thocht. He just aboot crippled me! I've never bin the same since.

Cheyne: Balderdash! It's rheumatics, pure an simple. Doctor Mackay...

Marni: What the hell dis thon ould quack know aboot anythin? I tell ye, he tried til kill me!

Cheyne: You poor deluded woman. You know, I wouldn't have blamed him if he had.

    Marni grunts

Henry: Marni, Hector wouldn't've hurt a fly.

Marni: (*turning on him*) Ye're such a gullable gapass, Henry, an ye're as slow as a broken clock.

Henry: (*losing his cool*) You arrogant old windbag! I've just about had enough o yer wild mouth. I swear I'll...

Shona: (*throwing herself on him*) Henry, it's no worth it!

Marni: (*to Henry*) Ye're under a Swanson roof, boy! If ye dinna lek it, skedaddle!

Shona: (*to Marni*) He's ma husband, damn yer eyes, an I'm as much a Swanson as ye!

Marni: (*laughing*) Shona, Shona, get rid o this sluan, an get yersel a real man.

Shona: Real, real? Oh, Marni. Reality seems til hev slipped far away frae ye.

Marni: (*almost hissing*) I know what I know!

Seoras: (*banging his fist on the table*) This has gone far enough! Will ye all shut up an show some respect for the death o a family member?

Cheyne: Well said.

Marni: He was a thief an a murderer! He tried til kill me, ye canna change that!

Seoras: So help me I'll kill ye if ye dinna shut up!

*Shona has collapsed weeping in **Henry**'s arms. He holds her, his face white, his limbs shaking. **Cheyne** swigs from his brandy glass, his brow narrow and heavy with sweat. **Marni** glowers at **Seoras** like a wolf at a lamb. He stares back at her, his features set with a sad resignation.*

Marni: (*muttered under her breath like a curse*) Fool!

Seoras: (*replying in similar manner*) Witch!

*Enter **Moira**, rather unsteadily.*

Moira: What the hell's goin on here? Aa they sheep-shaggers are wonderin where the family have got to. Ye'd better do somethin or they'll be eatin the carpets soon. (*pause*) What ye all lookin at? (*weakly*) Seoras?

Marni: Get that craitur oot o ma sicht.

Moira: (*stung back into her confident self*) C'mere ye ould crow, tae I batter yer puss!

*Seoras rushes across the room and catches **Moira** just before she unleashes a left hook in the direction of **Marni**'s head.*

Seoras: Hey, cut that oot. (*he throws her into a chair*) Now sit there an dinna say anither word. A that goes for everybody!

Moira: (*sarcastically*) Seoras, you're so masterful.

Seoras: Just shut the fuck up! (*there is a nervous silence*) There are important things wae hev til discuss an since we're all here, an at each ither's throats, as usual, in good ould Swanson style, wae micht as weel make a stab at it. Now, the central issue is this ferm an whether it'll be kept on or selt.

Marni: I'll never sell. Never!

Seoras: Ye're in no position til dictate what happens, Marni, so haud yer wheesht! The position is this: ye only hev one legal third an Shona an mysel hev two. An Marni, ye micht be my auntie but I dinna trust ye one inch! Which is why I want til get this discussion oot intil the open so everybody knows whit the score is.

Marni: Ye wid air Swanson family business in front o strangers?

Shona: There are no strangers here.

Seoras: Exactly.

Marni: (*trying to get out of the seat where she has slouched*) I'm no stayin here til listen til such trock.

Seoras: (*pushing her back down into her seat*) Ye are, an ye will! Now I want ye, for the first time in yer life, til tell me the truth. Are ye, or are ye no, plannin til sell Bunillidh Mains?

Marni: No.

Cheyne: Yes.

Marni: Traitor!

Seoras: So whit is it, Marni? Are ye, or are ye no?

Marni: Whit the hell d'ye know aboot fermin anyway! Ye've never grown up! Ye'll never understan the pain o it.

Seoras: I understan a swindle when I smell one.

Marni: This place is mine. I worked it. I earned it. I can do wae it whit I please!

Seoras: No ye canna! That's where ye're wrong. Ye've bin doin whit ye lek'd all yer life, but now, just for once, ye're goin til comply wae the wishes o the majority.

Marni: Phah! Dinna make me laugh!

Shona: Seoras, stop it! This is horrible.

Seoras: We hev til get til the bottom o this once an for all.

Shona: Henry, make him stop.

Henry: He's right, Shona, it has to be done. I'm sorry.

> *Shona tears herself away from Henry in disgust and stares moodily out of the window.*

Shona: (*mumbling to herself*) This is a hoose o death.

> *Henry follows her over*

Seoras: (*to Marni, leaning over her*) Are ye, or are ye no, plannin til sell?

> *There is no answer. Marni's face twitches.*

Seoras: Are ye, or are ye no, plannin til sell?

Marni: (*screaming*) Ay!! I'm sellin!!

Seoras: I knew it. At last.

Marni: Over yer heids! Behind yer backs! Whitever way ye lek it. There's nothin else for it! (*she starts to laugh*)

Seoras: Why no try imagination? Ye could make that work for ye.

Marni: No wae Doctor Death here. I know whit's comin, an it's the end o everythin. Wae canna fight, no any more. No against thon!

Shona: (*turning, tears in her eyes*) What? Tell us?

Cheyne: She can't, but I will. She sees the end of history coming. If these plans for a nuclear dump come to fruition – and they will, eventually, in some form or other – there will be nothing left here but heather and whin. Only the deer will converse and that in silence. We will be gone, our language not even a memory. Like Glen Loth we will be a beautiful bunch of rocks, some stones standing in God-alone-knows-what geometry. That's what she sees. (*to Shona*) If I did not hate her for her honesty I could love her for her sorrow.

Henry: You're all too in love with tragedy. Is there no fight left in you?

Marni: (*to Henry, under her breath*) Go back sooth til yer muck.

Seoras: (*kneeling before Marni*) Is the money so important? Marni, what's gone wrong?

Marni: (*softly*) I dinna know, Seoras, believe me but my stomach is a spree o adders.

Seoras: I hev no richt til judge ye, neither me nor Shona here. (*he takes Shona's hand*) We are the culpable ones, if there are any. Oh my girl, (*he touches Marni's cheek*) my grey aunt, we've wandered ower far, ower long. Forgive us.

Marni silently and slowly gets up from her seat and walks quietly off the stage. Shona cups her brother's head in her hands.

Shona: Put no blame against us, for no love nor luck can touch us amongst this blackness. Better til se the sea an the flat green land, it'll hold us a bonnie few ages yet.

Seoras: (*softly*) Wae hev til stay.

Shona: Nothin else.

Seoras: (*he hugs her*) If there's anythin left on this coast, then its oors.

Shona: There are the songs, Seoras, the songs o this grey coast hev hed many singers, many tunes. We're just anither set. We've forgotten, but we must remember.

Seoras: We will.

Suddenly a shot is heard

Cheyne: Marni!! (*he rushes offstage*)

Shona: (*screaming*) No!!

She rushes after Cheyne but Henry stops her

Henry: No, Shona, stay here.

Seoras: Blood, more blood.

Shona sinks to her knees

Henry: (*trying to console her*) Shona, we must leave here.

Moira rises from her seat where she has been observing all that has been going on. She crosses to Seoras.

Moira: Seoras, ye're wastin yer time. It's hopeless.

Seoras: (*weakly*) No.

Enter Cheyne. There is blood on his hands.

Cheyne: She's dead.

Seoras and Shona cling to each other

Cheyne: There's nothing you can do for her now. The shotgun she… well…

Henry: We'd better call the police.

Cheyne: My dear boy I *am* the police! No one must go through there, not for anything, I urge you. Everything must be left exactly as it is for the pathologist.

Henry: What about the funeral guests. They…

Cheyne: Wouldn't have heard a thing. The walls here are four feet thick. I'll deal with them in a minute.

Moira: She's safe now.

Shona: Safe? What d'ye mean?

Moira: I mean safe from youz bastards!

Henry: Why can't you stop this feuding?

Seoras: Ye poor gowk, can ye no see the feud is at its hicht? Through in the scullery lies anither casualty.

Henry: (*at the end of his tether*) You people are your own worst enemy. If you'd stop fighting amongst yourselves and concentrate on the real problems you might be able to do something about it!

Seoras: Henry.
Henry: What?
Seoras: Fuck off!

> *Seoras punches **Henry** squarely on the face. **Henry** tumbles to the ground. **Shona**, who was being consoled by **Cheyne**, breaks free from him and runs to **Henry**.*

Shona: Seoras, ye're an animal.

> *She dabs a handkerchief onto **Henry**'s bleeding lip.*

Henry: (*almost weeping*) I'm okay, I'm okay.
Shona: No ye're no, stay still.
Seoras: Henry, I'm sorry, I…
Moira: Ach, Seoras, shut up. Ye're no sorry, ye meant it. (*she puts her arms around him*) Must say, I didnae think ye had it in ye. (*she kisses him*)
Cheyne: Well, I suppose I'd better go and tell everyone the ceilidh's over. They'll be wondering what the hell's going on. Must say, I wonder myself. Seoras, we must talk. If you plan to stay there are things that need to be done. I'd run your hand under the tap if I were you, or your mitt will swell up like a neep.

> *Cheyne exits. **Henry** manages to get to his feet.*

Henry: Shona, we're leaving.
Shona: No, Henry, I'm no goin anywhere.
Henry: (*dumbfounded*) But you can't stay here now!
Shona: Now especially.
Henry: If I leave here on my own, then this relationship is over.
Shona: Ach, Henry, it wis over ages ago. I just couldnae see it, that's all.
Henry: (*furious*) You stupid woman!

> *Henry exits. **Shona** stands till, staring ahead as if in a trance. **Seoras** moves over to her and addresses her with all the respect and tenderness he can muster.*

Seoras: Ye can go after him if ye lek. There's still a chance, ye know. I'll understan.
Shona: Henry's no for me, no any more. Naa, Seoras, from now on I'm goin til stan my easel under a northern sky. I'm goin til paint a face back ontil this coast. At last, at last, I'm alive.

Scene Three

It is the following morning. The kitchen is in an untidy state. The residue of the previous day's events lie about the place. Glasses, bottles, plates, half-eaten sandwiches, cakes and so on. Chairs sit askew. The table stands as though it too has a hangover.

*Enter **Blacksmith**. He wanders around for a minute or two, poking at this and that, picking things up to examine them, much as an anthropologist would do in some far-off and distant desert island where there lived a forgotten people with an unknown civilisation. He turns and faces the audience.*

Blacksmith: The sun has come out at last. The sudden gales have stopped and with them the hailstones. The skylarks are singing and the gorse, or should I say whin, is in its coconut bloom. The lambs grow ever more plentiful and gambol upon the links and the valley, or should I say 'strath', like... well, lambs.

And I used to think that not much could ever possibly happen here! Well? Each day it gets brighter and the light hangs longer in the evening sky. And what light! Pale and gentle and so low it makes the flat land even flatter and the high brown mountains even higher. I have never, in all my travellings, seen anything quite like it. One feels time seeping out from the sea onto the land and into one's very inner being. This place is as much inscape as it is landscape. The coast makes words seem like so many superfluous raindrops.

And of the people who speak them – oh, what is one to make of them? They are like no species I have ever encountered before. They seem to laugh at death, yet they are not savages. Not entirely. But their lives appear as raw as the weather and their hostility to my vocation and purpose is a vexing hurdle I'm not sure I can overcome. Reason seems to have no place in their make-up. The more I tell them about the safe nature of the Authority's plans the more they disbelieve me. The more I try to convince them of the infallibility of nuclear physics and of the advanced state of our engineering the more they shake their heads and say they don't know. But *I* know. *I* know! In the name of reason, what am I to do?

*Enter **Shona***

Shona: Ye could begin by tellin yersel the truth, that ye're no infallible.
Blacksmith: (*turning*) Good morning, Mrs Henderson, I didn't hear you come in.
Shona: Ye're no a God, Doctor Blacksmith, ye're no in control o life an death, although ye'd lek til be. (*she sits down*)
Blacksmith: I must say I'm stunned with the appalling nature of recent events. Miss Swanson was a remarkable woman. She... well, you must be shattered.
Shona: Shattered? That's the least o it. We must let the stoor settle, Doctor, which is why yer presence is so unsettling.

Blacksmith: Let me put your mind at rest on that score. I have just returned for the rest of my things and will be out of the house shortly.

Shona: It's no just here, it's this entire coast ye're ruinin. Be gone, man.

Blacksmith: I've just about had enough of this. If you are about to launch into some pompous moral rant against something you know nothing about and don't understand then I assure you, Mrs Henderson, I will not be listening.

Shona: Your kind never listen.

Blacksmith: But it is you who do not listen. I am tired of defending my science against mere superstition and ignorance.

Shona: I'm no criticising yer scientific or personal integrity, doctor. But yer paymasters are no quite so honest as ye. They play politics wae oor futures. Weel, let me tell ye: politics failed this coast ower two hunner years ago. We can see through a bloody lie when we're told it.

Blacksmith: Politics is not my concern.

Shona: How convenient.

Blacksmith: My employers have nothing to gain from deception. I honestly believe that.

Shona: Ye peedie bairn. Tell me, are ye married?

Blacksmith: Yes, I've been married for over twenty years.

Shona: Bairns?

Blacksmith: I have two children. A boy of sixteen and a fourteen-year-old girl.

Shona: Are they happy?

Blacksmith: James and Virginia? Yes, yes I think they are.

Shona: An yer family are in England, I suppose?

Blacksmith: Yes. We live in Middlesex.

Shona: An they're comfortable? I mean, ye'll hev a good hoose?

Blacksmith: I'd like to think I've always ensured their comfort.

Shona: D'ye think they'd be comfortable if they lived on this grey coast?

Blacksmith: Yes, I'm almost certain. It's so very beautiful.

Shona: Ay, an poor. Yer bairns'd hev til learn til be comfortable here, Doctor, they'd hev til learn til be poor, they'd hev til be able til live wae no future prospects, nothin. D'ye think they could handle that?

Blacksmith: You are altogether too bleak.

Shona: Doctor, wae all due respect, whit d'ye really know aboot it? Ye're only here til survey this coast. So, alright, ye've fallen in love wae her, an ye'll no be that last soothmoother til dae that, for this coast hes her charms alricht. But the Nuclear Authority dinna gie a tuppenny damn for her or her folk. They want til bury their poisonous filth in her belly an leave it festerin there for thousands o years. An it's the location o the belly that's important. They've bin coverin up for ower thirty year the leaks an cock-ups at thon reactor along the coast. But what d'ye ken o that?

Blacksmith: It's not my field. But I have every confidence…

Shona: Go home, Doctor, I beg ye. Tell them this land isna suitable for their dump. (*she rises from her chair*) Tell them anythin.

Blacksmith: I will present the findings of my survey. I will tell them the truth.

Shona: The truth? The truth's a deid scorrie on the beach. The truth's my auntie wae a shotgun burn where her heid used til be. Tell them aboot Marni, Doctor, if ye want til tell the truth.

Blacksmith: If a waste re-processing plant is sited here I have applied for the post of safety inspector. I have been led to believe from unofficial sources that I will be given that post.

Shona: Ye are one man. By that time the Nuclear Authority will be a private company whose main concern'll be profit.

Blacksmith: Again, that is politics and no concern of mine. You think of me as an uncaring mercenary and the Authority as hit and run merchants. That is unfair.

Shona: (*she approaches him*) Ye're a good man, Doctor, a sincere man. On that score I hev nae doots.

> *She cups his head in her hands. Her voice, her stature, her face now seem to have taken on an archaic quality, as though all the women of the grey coast from all time are speaking through her now. She has become the grey coast.*

Shona: But go now, go from this place an no harm will come til ye or any o yer people. Here oor sorrows must heal an oor hearts find their joy once more. Go now, for I am deep in dream. Go now, an take my blessin wae ye.

> *She kisses him slowly, deeply and gently on the mouth, as if she is transferring her intentions, her will, her magic over to him.* **Blacksmith** *stands still, overcome with shock as if he is now possessed. He tries to speak but* **Shona** *raises her hand to quieten him. She is herself again.*

Shona: Shhh. No words. For ye til stay wid wake her, an if she wakens she'll destroy ye. So go. Go.

> *Confused, upset and visibly moved, his eyes full of tears, his hands shaking,* **Blacksmith** *stumbles off. He is a man unsure of himself now, as if his purpose has slid from him like a sheet off an old chair, his anxiety sparking off him like electricity.*

> *Enter* **Cheyne**

Cheyne: What on earth's wrong with Doctor Death? He looks like a man gone over the edge. What exactly have you been doing with him, my young lady?

Shona: I hevna been doin anythin wae him, I assure ye.

Cheyne: Oh come, come, my dear. A woman such as yourself and a man such as Doctor Blacksmith? Well, I mean, it's no wonder he looks like a scalded cat!

Shona: I just canna think whit ye mean.

*She starts tidying things up. **Cheyne** runs his eye over her.*

Cheyne: Well, I can, by golly.

Shona: I wis merely pointin oot til the Doctor the error o his ways an the damaging nature o his enterprise, an that he should go home til the sooth as soon as he can.

Cheyne: Oh I see, a mere trifle. Well, it's no wonder he's looking so deliriously happy.

Shona: Have they finished? Is she comin home?

Cheyne: It'll be a day or two yet, I'm afraid. Post mortems take forever. They do them all in Inverness these days. Poor Marni.

Shona: Ye loved her, did ye no?

Cheyne: Love? I don't know what the word means. But Marni had a certain something. Anyway, she wasn't interested in men; not that way.

Shona: I know. Sometimes I wonder whit she *wis* interested in?

Cheyne: Cattle, mainly. She's the only woman I've ever known who fell in love with a bull!

Shona: (*laughing*) That's right. I remember. Roddy, that wis his name. He won two Highland Shows, did he no?

Cheyne: That he did. You know she was offered a God's own price for him, but no, she wasn't selling. Love is lord of all. Marni; she was one and one only. I'll miss her, quite frankly.

The Swanston Kitchen.

*There is a strong sense of tears in **Cheyne**'s eyes. **Shona** notices.
But true to his stoic principles: Sheriffs don't cry.*

Shona: (*ushering him into a seat*) Oh, Struan, sit doon. I'll make some tea. Ye'll feel better.

Cheyne: (*sitting*) Thanks, but I'll have no tea. I don't feel like anything much.

Shona: A brandy?

Cheyne: Well, perhaps just a wee one for comfort.

> ***Shona** laughs and moves over to the press and pours a drink for **Cheyne**. She hands him the glass.*

Cheyne: God bless you, my dearest girl. (*he throws it down in one*) Well, that's them all away now. It's strange.

Shona: They'll never leave though, this hoose is full o shadows.

Cheyne: Still, you're staying.

Shona: (*softly*) Ay.

Cheyne: Well, you are, aren't you?

Shona: (*she hugs herself as if she is cold*) Oh Struan, I dinna know.

Cheyne: (*concerned*) But I was under the impression that yourself and Seoras had come round to the idea.

Shona: I canna speak for Seoras, although I never imagined him as a farmer, but as for mysel, weel... ach, I dinna want til lose this place, but I've got things til do, Struan, pictures til paint, places til see. Aaaargh! I canna explain it!

Cheyne: There's no need. I understand. You're an artist and the world's your canvas. I admire that. I wish there were more like you.

Shona: (*moving behind his chair*) Ye, Struan Cheyne, Sheriff o Bunillidh? surely never?

Cheyne: You can mock, but once I had aspirations to be an actor. Thought I felt the call of the greasepaint and the boards. But it wasn't to be. So I've been acting the fool in the courtroom ever since. Plenty drama there. But one can dream. You have dreams too, my darling girl, so you follow them. Leave these old fields and cliffs to the likes of Seoras and myself. If you don't what are we? Just dumb men with no poetry in our blood.

Shona: (*she stroke his hair affectionately*) Ye ould sweetie thing.

Cheyne: Careful, my girl, old volcanoes are the most dangerous.

> ***Shona** laughs, throwing her head back. He softly touches her neck.*

Cheyne: Whatever happened to that husband of yours? Left kind of suddenly, didn't he?

Shona: (*moving away across the stage to the window*) Let's just say we hed come til the end o a journey. It's sad, I s'pose, but it hed til be. Bein here, wae whit's happened, just brocht it all til a head. I'm grateful for that, Struan, I really am.

Cheyne: That's good. Everything here has a way of making sense eventually.

Shona: The tide comes in, then it goes out again. (*she spins round*) But ye mustna dwell on things! Never!

Cheyne: (*rising from his seat*) Well, neither must I any longer. I just came over to see if there was anything you needed.

Shona: We're fine.

> Enter **Seoras** and **Moira**, *who for the first time in the play is sober and not suffering from a hangover.*

Seoras: (*full of energy*) Ahcourse we are! An whit's the rush, Struan, ye ould dug?

Cheyne: None much, save for the affairs of the Sheriff's office.

Seoras: Ye mean the lounge bar o Sinclair's Hotel, eh?

Cheyne: (*smiling*) I might.

Shona: (*to Seoras*) Struan's bin very kind. There's no need til be so rude.

Moira: (*to Shona*) Seoras thinks he's a farmer now.

Seoras: An so I am.

Moira: Whether ye lek it or no.

Seoras: (*he tickles her in the ribs*) I lek it, I lek it!

Moira: (*to no-one in particular*) He's been like this all mornin. It's drivin me demented.

Shona: (*to Moira softly*) Ye see, hae's got no brain. (*the two women laugh conspiratorially*)

Seoras: (*to Cheyne*) Whit the hell's the matter wae Blacksmith? I saw him tearin off doon the A9 lek a mad hare.

Cheyne: I think your sister put the heebiejeebies on him.

Seoras: She aye wis a bit o a feeach, Shona. Got it off oor Grannie. (*to Shona*) Ye bin makin the mannie's milk to thin then, eh?

Shona: (*almost blushing*) I hev no.

Moira: Well, ye'd need somethin pretty special tae make thon man go thick.

Seoras: D'ye hear that, Struan, it said "thon".

Moira: I never did.

Cheyne: Stranger things have happened, Mrs Swanson, stranger things. (*he casts a furtive glance towards Shona*)

> **Seoras**, *mimicking a ghost, chases* **Moira** *around the table.*

Seoras: Whoooooooooooh!!

Moira: Get away wae ye!

Cheyne: So what about the rigs, Seoras? What's going to happen there?

Seoras: (*stopping*) Next trip I go back I hand in my notice. I'll just say "Sorry but I changed my mind".

Shona: Seoras, are ye sure?

Seoras: As sure as I'm goin til be a father.

Shona: (*bemused*) Moira, is this...?

Moira: Fraid so. My mother aye told me no tae sleep wae my knees up. Guess I got pissed once too often.

Shona: (*she begins to dance with excitement*) Oh, this is beautiful, so beautiful. Oh, Seoras, ye sneaky devil!

Seoras: Hey hey, it was all planned, I assure ye.

Shona: Oh Moira, I'm so happy.

Moira: Ye hev it then.

Cheyne: (*shaking Seoras by the hand*) Congratulations, old man. Well done. This calls for a drink.

Seoras: No time, Struan, there's a ewe heavy oot there at the top o the three-cornered park. C'mon Moira, let's see if we can get ye some tips!

Moira: Tips? If ye think ye're havin me delivered lek ye did thon last lamb, ye've got another think comin!

Seoras: Ye see? "Thon". She said it again. (*he chases Moira offstage*) C'mon ma puddag, or it's a deid ewe we'll be havin.

> *Moira screams in mock horror. They both exit.*

Cheyne: I don't think I've ever seen such a change come over a man.

Shona: Ye know, for once, I think Seoras is happy.

Cheyne: And the wild woman?

Shona: Moira? Her too. She's goin til be a mither. Why shouldna she be happy?

Cheyne: Ah, happiness. How many of us can say we are truly happy?

> *Shona considers what Cheyne has said, and she speaks as though she has thought about what she is going to say for a thousand years.*

Shona: I dunno, but I believe I've got the potential for it inside o me. Wae all hev, no?

Cheyne: You are such a beautiful thing, so I suppose it's the duty of this cynical old man to believe you.

Shona: (*the look of the feeach comes back into her eyes*) Oh exactly. If we could marry happiness wae belief, Struan, whit a weddin that wid be!

Cheyne: A pleasant thought, that. You see, Shona, the tide may go out for a while, but it comes back in again, as sure as the moon.

Shona: (*smiling*) C'mon, Struan, come an look at Seoras's ewe afore ye go back til the office.

Cheyne: Well, why not? The sheep shite will hide the smell of the brandy.

Shona: (*laughing*) Ye ould rogue.

Cheyne: (*as they are about to exit*) By the way, old girl, what exactly did you say to Doctor Death?

> *Shona stops for a moment. She thinks about it. She smiles. For a moment it looks as though she will spill the beans, but she thinks better of it. She looks at Cheyne and in her eyes are still the songs of the grey coast. She laughs. But then she whispers...*

Shona: Oh, nothin...

> *Cheyne for once in his life is totally puzzled. He looks at Shona with respect and amazement. He gently puts his arm around her shoulders. They exit.*

The End

The Gold of Kildonan

First performed by

Eden Court Theatre Company

at

Kildonan Hall

3rd October 1989

Aslief... Vari Sylvester

Seoras Mackay ....Hugh Loughlan

Catriona Mackay ....Lisa Grindall

Meg Mackay/Broath ....Kay Gallie

Sandy Grand/Bridei ....Iain Wotherspoon

P D Sinclair/Donnan ....Matthew Zajac

Donald Mackay/Peacock .... Billy Riddoch

Musician.. Andy Thorburn

Director .... Catherine Robins

Designer...Simon Fraser

Composer.. Donald Shaw

Stage Manager ....Lorna Morrison

DSM..Mary Ann marshall

ASM (acting) ....Kevin McEwen

Wardrobe supervisor..Moira Bromley-Wiggins

Wardrobe Assistant...Sheila Toner

Tour Organiser ....Mairi MacIver

Tour Administrator... David Meek

This play is dedicated to the good people of Kildonan, or
Ullie, and to the good folk of Helmsdale, or Bunillidh.

The Gold of Kildonan

Cast

Seoras Mackay, a gold digger
Catriona Mackay, his wife
Donald Mackay, a fisherman and father of Seoras
Meg Mackay, the wife of Donald Mackay
Sandy Grant, a fisherman turned gold digger
Peter Dominicus Sinclair, a jeweller
Peacock, a factor
Aslief, a feeach – or witch – or shaman
Broath, a creature of myth
Bridei, a Pictish Mormaer, or chief
Donnan, a Celtic Catholic missionary from Ireland

Set

The play is set in Strath Ulliean, Sutherland, in 1869 (except for Act I Scene 2 which is set in the Otago River valley in New Zealand). The play is based on the gold rush which occurred in Strath Kildonan in 1868/9. The characters in the play, however, are fictitious but any resemblances to persons either living or dead is highly desirable.

Note on the language

The language of the play, if it were to be absolutely accurate, would be Gaelic throughout. The indication must be that the characters *are* speaking Gaelic naturally, with the exception of Peacock and Sinclair where it would be their second language – if they ever spoke it at all. But of course the characters are *not* speaking Gaelic so the actors must attempt a Highland setting without resorting to the "neffer" and "effer" of the stage Highlander. I would rather the play was intoned in Received Pronunciation. Also it must *never* be done in southern Scots.

George Gunn 1989

Act I

"Dreams in a pan..."

Scene One

*Bare stage. Music is heard. Enter **Aslief**, a feeach or witch. She is accompanied by **Broath**, a serpent.*

Aslief: In the beginning was the song
and the song was of gold
and through the turning centuries
the song it did unfold
through fire, through water
through the shaking air
the song became the world
and the world I did ensnare

I am Aslief, feeach of these northern straths
My mother was the golden moon
my father the silver mountain wolf
The distant future for me is soon
All human ways are known to me
My voice is a joining thread of gold
My home is the summit of Ben Griam
My dreams are new songs for the old

Broath: I am Broath, guardian of this world
and all its folk
I was born in its fiery heart
that is both light and dark
Beneath Cnoc na Beiste
I have made my home,
in Strath Ulliean of the golden spark
My breath sleeps beneath the stone

Aslief: Broath watched amid the rocks
She sleeps deep beneath the hill
She dreams the music of the burns
of Ulliean, Helmsdale, of Suisgill
Her body is long and twisting
Her shape is that of the strath
from Cnoc an Eireannaich to Creag Dal-Langal

Broath: Time does not sit easily on Cnoc a'Mheadoin
Metal hands cut into my side
the hungry ones on Creag Druim nan Rath
great need have they for my fire, my blood
Evening has come to kiss Strath Ulliean
Sadness from my eyes turns to water

flowing down the centuries to Allt Duibhe
I guard Strath Ulliean, my golden mother
Gold is not for mere usury
Wealth is not for individual gain
whether prince's crown or chieftain's teeth
the strath her riches must retain
for the good and gift of all
I, Broath, tell you this
My form in rock and golden grain
from the earth's burning heart I hiss

Aslief: Strath Ulliean mourns her children's passing
Her true riches now have gone
Donan's words no longer fill the soul
Bridei's tongue graces Bannerman and Gunn
Mackay and Keith, all now of distant shores
I, Aslief, foretold of their going
My blood is Alchemy of Gàidhlig and Norn
My twin visions are all-seeing, all-knowing

Broath: Anger, anger, anger!
I know your iron name
Gold

Aslief: Seek, ye fools, your undoing
here where greed is shame
Gold!

Broath: Magnetite
Aslief: Titaniferous
Broath: Almandine garnet
Aslief: Hornblende
Broath: Rutile
Aslief: Tourmaline
Broath: Zircon
Aslief: Epidote
Broath: Quartz
Aslief: Feldspar
Broath: Greed, greed, greed
I know your iron name
Aslief & Broath: Gold!

Aslief: These then are the angels
of a dead universe
They lie with Broath
under Cnoc na Beiste
and the golden blood of Strath Ulliean
I, Aslief, tell you this is so
with fortune as misfortune's tryst
and time alone know

They exit. Music.

Scene Two

*A riverbank on the Otago River, New Zealand. **Seoras** and **Catriona** are prospecting for gold. She is digging with a rough wooden spade, he is panning.*

Catriona: Must we always be digging in the dirt for a living?

Seoras: What else would ye hev us do, Catriona? Work like a dog on one o those sheep stations up around Dunedin?

Catriona: A body can make an honest wage there. It's a fine town, Seoras, made from stone. A real place. No like those wooden towns ye see all over the place. Oh, Seoras, we should know where we are!

Seoras: But we know where we are. This is the Otago river. The South Island. New Zealand.

Catriona: New Zealand. Dinna I just know it.

Seoras: Weel, what's wrong wae it all o a sudden?

Catriona: Ach, there's no folk here, Seoras, no a soul we can speak til. No in Gàidhlig anyway. Thon English just doesna seem til fit my mouth.

Seoras: It's a problem, I know.

Catriona: In Dunedin there are lots o folk like us. Sutherland folk. Caithnessians too.

Seoras: Caithnessians! Then by God we'll no be going there!

Catriona: Seoras!

Seoras: (*mimicking her*) Catriona!

Catriona laughs a little but reverts into her sadness.

Catriona: I'm tired o this.

Seoras: (*he stops panning*) I know, I know. But we've only got another few feet till the end o the stake, an that'll be that.

Catriona: (*she leans on her spade*) That's no what I meant. I'm tired o living in a tent. I'm tired o cooking out o the one pot. I'm tired o wandering along endless rivers an valleys. Ach, I'm just plain tired.

He moves over to her.

Seoras: But we're doing away. We've money in the bank. No a fortune, I'll admit, but claims are easy til find an cheap til stake. The work is hard, I'll grant ye, but the gold willna jump out at ye singing "Here, here I am!"

Catriona: Ye said we would make our fortune. That nuggets the size o yer fist were just lying around waiting til be found. That's what ye said! Weel, where are they, Seoras? We've never found any.

Seoras: Did ye really think it would be like that? Is that what ye expected?

Catriona: What d'ye take me for, man, a fool? But maybe I didna expect it til be so difficult.

Seoras: Ach, who said it was going til be easy? If we keep at it we'll make out. Oh Catriona, ye have til keep at it. Ye canna give up. Ye an me, we can do it. We dinna go intil the towns an spend our dust on rum an brandy. We dinna live it up in the new hotels!

Catriona: Weel, maybe we should! What I wouldna give for a hot bath.

Seoras: There's a hot spring just ten miles over the north ridge. Ye can bathe there.

Catriona: What? In the open, like an animal?

Seoras: (*trying not to laugh*) It's just for now. Later, ye can have all the hot baths ye want. Or anything else ye have a mind for. We've been over it a hundred times.

Catriona: Ay, that we have. But we never spoke o living like animals. Three years, Seoras, three long years o digging, sluicing, panning, dreaming. (*pause*) Ye could make more at the sheep stations.

Seoras: Would ye have me be a slave til another man? An with sheep? Covered in ticks and lice? My God we crossed the world til escape that! Sheep, sheep, sheep! I'm haunted by infernal sheep. I ask nothing o no man, an I expect nothing. Sheriffs' warrants an eviction notices are all that expectancy ever gave us. I thought those times were over! I thought we were free!!

Catriona: (*not listening*) We go on an on an on. An I'm tired, oh so tired. For all yer talk o freedom I feel as though I'm dying here. Oh Seoras, I dinna want til die here.

Pause

Seoras: Look, ye take over the pan for a bit. I'll do the digging.

Catriona: (*resuming her digging*) Ach, ye know fine I'm no good at it. I havena got yer eye. I'd just lose us any gold that's there.

Seoras: Then we'll finish for the day. The sun's getting low anyway. I'll have til gather up some more wood, though. It'll be cold the night by the look o that sky.

Catriona: (*she puts her spade down*) What a strange country this is. So unbearably hot in the day, an so terribly cold at night. A body can hardly thole it.

Seoras: Just listen til ye, ye'd think it was hell itself ye were describing.

Catriona: Sometimes I think hell could be little worse than this.

Seoras: (*putting his arms around her*) Ach, Catriona, what is it that gnaws away at ye like this? It's no as if we're starving. We're better off than most other gold diggers we know. An ye canna tell me ye've suddenly shied off hard work? No, my Catriona. So why all this disquiet, eh? What's really behind it?

Catriona: Ach, ye'll laugh at me for my stupidness.

Seoras: (*mimicking her*) Ach, I will no. Now will ye be telling me?

She moves across the stage.

Catriona: Seoras, look at these hills. Look at the way they gently rise from the river bed. Look how they seem til caress the sky. Just look at the colour an shape o them!

Seoras: Ay, I'm looking.

Catriona: Look at these rocks, these stones. Dinna they remind ye o anything?

Seoras: Ay, they remind me o the last four valleys we've dug in, an the other four that lie round that river bend.

Catriona: Ach, ye've been away too long! They're like home, Seoras, like Strath Ulliean. Canna ye see it?

Seoras: (*pensively*) Now that ye mention it, I suppose there is a slight resemblance.

Catriona: Slight, he says. Slight! Why for the past two weeks it's been whispering til me, tugging away at my mind.

Seoras: What, what has?

Catriona: Home, that's what. Home. Strath Ulliean. Sutherland. Oh, Seoras, I want til go home!

Seoras: Home! Och now I know yer havering! We canna go back. We came here til go forward, til progress.

Catriona: Til progress? What progression is this? We're at the bottom, an we're going til stay at the bottom until our hands turn til bony claws. We came across the sea til escape. But we canna escape!

Seoras: But til go back home, it's impossible.

Catriona: It's no impossible. We've enough money. Ye said so yersel.

Seoras: I said we'd saved more than most other diggers. But why waste our money on expensive trips just because ye're homesick? An have ye plain forgotten why exactly it was we came here til New Zealand, eh? Weel, have ye?

Catriona: (*sadly*) No, I havena.

Seoras: An has it slipped yer mind that both our families were evicted, their houses burned over their heads? Or that they were forced til live in a series o brick huts they call Helmsdale?

Catriona: No, Seoras, I havena forgotten anything. That's the whole point.

Seoras: It's these hills. They've made ye nostalgic. Go home indeed. An what til? The poverty? Til my father's shouting? Or is it the fishing ye're harking after? Would ye have me drowned for the sake o a few herring?

Catriona: I surely wouldna.

Seoras: Weel, what's all this talk, then? We've made about seven pounds this week already, an it's only Thursday.

Catriona: That's what I mean. (*she picks up a rock*) Look at this rock. What d'ye see?

He examines it.

Seoras: It's a good rock. A bit o quartz in it. Sound proof there's gold in the river. That's why we're here.

Catriona: There are rocks like this in Strath Ulliean, Seoras, we played over them as bairns. The hillsides are made o them. Ye know that fine.

Seoras: What exactly are ye saying?

Catriona: Remember the stories we were told? O the Irishman who made gold from beneath the hill? O the golden warrior? O the gold in King David's crown? Gold from Strath Ulliean, Seoras, gold from rocks just like this!

Seoras: Stories, Catriona, just stories.

Catriona: An I suppose there are no stories about Otago then? I suppose the Maoris have no legends about these hills, these rocks?

Seoras: Who knows what these heathens concoct. I hear tell they eat white folk.

Catriona: An who can blame them?

Seoras: Catriona, what evil is this ye're condoning?

Catriona: It's these hills, Seoras, they could easily be Strath Ulliean! An the black folk, ay, I've seen them stare at us. I saw some this morning.

Seoras: For goodness sake, ye should've said! I'll have til carry the gun now.

Catriona: Ye'll do no such thing! What have we become here? At home we stared at the factors an the sheep farmers in much the same way. We looked upon them with hate. Or have *ye* forgotten? The same hate the black man has when he looks at us. Oh, Seoras! This morning, when I saw them on the hills, I knew we were doing wrong.

Seoras: An what wrong are we doing here exactly? Our claims are legally granted from Wellington.

Catriona: What does it matter to the folk on the hill? Their claims are written in time. Just as ours were in Strath Ulliean. We were dispossessed. Now we're the dispossessors. We're Gaels, Seoras, must we bring destruction with us?

Seoras moves away from her. After a pause:

Seoras: D'ye think it's never crossed my mind? D'ye think I'm so hard that I dinna feel it too? But we canna afford it, Catriona. What pity we have left we should reserve for oursels. There are casualties in every age an I'm damned if I'm going til be one! As til the Maoris, they'll have til learn survival, just as we've had til learn.

Catriona: Then we're no better than the factors! They should come down from the hillsides an kill us all now! The sooner the better!

Seoras: Hey lassie, ye've a wild tongue in ye! An such a big heart. So is it any wonder that I love ye?

Catriona: Then let's stop this robbing. (*Seoras tries to embrace her but she avoids him*) An stop trying til change the subject.

Seoras: Is that what ye think o me? A robber is it?

Catriona: Ach, Seoras Mackay, ye havena got the brains til rob anybody.

Seoras: Why must we give up our independence? For that's what it would mean. Here the wind and the weather are our governor. The river is our only true friend. Oh, Catriona, what else can we do?

Catriona: (*staring at the rock*) We can go home. This rock tells me so. We can do what we're doing now in Strath Ulliean. We can dig for gold there.

Seoras: But the stories o gold are just that – stories!

Catriona: But with yer skill we can try. They say ye're the best panner in the South Island. We can make a go o it.

Seoras: Who says?

Catriona: What?

Seoras: That I'm the best panner in the South Island?

Catriona: (*teasing*) Och an wouldna ye just like til know? If I was til tell ye yer cap wouldna fit yer head.

Seoras: What ye say, I must confess, has its attractions. A bit romantic, but attractive none the less. Kind o like yersel. (*his mood changes*) But it's all so risky. Nobody's done it afore.

Catriona: Look, I'll make a deal with ye. (*she points*) Ye see that hill over there?

Seoras: Ay.

Catriona: Does it no look like Cnoc an Eireannaich?

Seoras: Weel, it does have a certain similarity.

Catriona: Let's go there an clasp hands. I promise ye that if we find nothing in Strath Ulliean, if the gold proves illusive an the stones false, I'll no squabble about returning here. But we must give it a year. An when we're in Strath Ulliean, under Cnoc an Eireannaich, we'll clasp hands again an swear the same thing. Will ye promise me that?

Seoras: An this'll make ye happy?

Catriona: It'll go a bit towards it. I canna explain it, Seoras, I just feel it. I've stuck with ye these past long years an I've asked for nothing. Ach, that's nothing much I'll admit but I ask ye this thing, just once. On our love for each other, will ye agree til it?

Seoras: Oh *mo leannan**, what else can I do?

Catriona: Ye'll no regret it, I promise ye. Oh, ye're well loved, Seoras Mackay

Seoras: On that I dinna doubt. But listen, ye must agree til return if there's no gold til be found. It's easy til say these things now but it may prove more difficult once ye're home. Yer blood is in Strath Ulliean.

Catriona: Oh I'll keep my side o it, dinna ye worry.

Seoras: (*almost to himself*) But, ye know, it will be good til see the old place again. I never thought I would.

Catriona: Remember, Seoras, we do it from love. It's time we repossessed our own land.

Seoras: An dinna get carried away. It's certain that we'll meet with opposition. It may prove difficult til get permission. Dinna expect the factors til share yer notions. I canna see them having softened any.

---

* my love

Catriona: We'll never know until we try. Surely it's better til try an fail at home than here on these poor people's land, an them no different from us save for the colour o their skin.

Seoras: My, my. Are ye no the marvellous one? D'ye think I should stick a bone through my nose then?

Catriona: Maybe it would make an improvement.

He feels his nose absent-mindedly.

Seoras: Ay, maybe it would at that. But come on now, afore ye have me agreeing til anything else. By God, ye'll have me farming next.

Catriona: Now that truly *would* be a sight! (*she holds the small of her back*) Ooh, ye know, I just might try that spring.

Seoras: Ay, why no? We can both wash off New Zealand.

They pick up their gear and exit. Music.

Scene Three

*Enter **Aslief** and **Bridei**, a Pictish Mormaer or Chieftain. They are carrying a dead man. Music throughout.*

Aslief: Long before the naming of names
I, Aslief, spun my golden thread
in the morning of the present
under the shadow of the future dead
and put war between man and man
to see that one survives
and watch ideas rise like new baked bread
and feed conflict into their lives

They lay the body down.

Bridei: I, Bridei, Mormaer of the Picti
bury my brother, Brude MacMaelchon
dead from a broken sword at Dunbaitte
here in Strath Ulliean, under Cnoc nam Feinn
by the Suisgill burn and Helmsdale water
Brude, slayer of Priest and Norseman
his blood flows red and golden
here in Strath Ulliean, where our lives catch the Sun

Aslief: Bridei was my last special child
His people's champion in Time's fresh shiver
when cat and bear and wolf sang in Strath Ulliean
and my voice heard in mountain and river
before my body graced the earth plane
Before Christian came, before the Viking
before the clack of the Angle oppressor
Bridei's teeth flashed golden and striking

*Exit **Aslief**. Enter **Donnan**, an Irish priest of the Celtic Catholic Church. **Bridei** is kneeling over his dead brother.*

Donnan: Your days are numbered, pagan
All your kind will end up like him

Indicating body

for Time has caught you by the tail
and whatever light you hold grows dim
Your people's needs have outgrown your fables
The voice of Christ whispers in their ears
His grace grows golden as yours grows grim
Your ways disappear down a tunnel of years

Bridei: (*rising*) Christian, why have you come here?
You bring a destruction with your sorcery
I have no quarrel with this Christ of yours
so why does he turn my people from me?
Your ways are foreign, feign and fickle

Aslief

You fill our hearts with guilt and fear
and make us dependent when once we were free
I should kill you now the air to clear
Donnan: If you do then I die a saint
and others come after me for I am not alone
Fergus, Cormack, Ninian, Drostan, Mungo
From Ireland we have come your sins to atone
We bring love and light and the word of God
for you, Bridei, and all your children
here to the hills of the golden stone
in these straths so rich and northern
Bridei: Episcopus Scotiae Pictus, I know your cant
Flatter on as much as you like, dreamer
I know the sham and shimmer of your game
Here we take our grace from hill and river
the wind, the tide, the rain, these our rosary
so what use to us is a man on a cross?
Your chants and beads betray your matter
To put us down, your gain – our loss
Donnan: Bridei, Bridei, have you no trust left?
The love of God through Christ is my message
all meat and matter melded there
Your hills and streams hold the devil's passage
and to Hell you will surely go
if you persist in these cruel dreams
but God is forgiving and I as his word's carriage
tell you that it is not as it seems
Bridei: Tell it to Brude, dead as he is
in the hall of heroes and visions
Your God will take our land
and build cold stone prisons
and wrap our hearts in thankless ceremony
and priests such as you will steal our tongue
Behind your cloak lie merchants' missions
We are old here, priest, we have grown wise and young

    Enter Aslief

Aslief: Bridei, they are as a tide
and you cannot push against them
Let them spread their religion
but your heart is not to blame
Come to me, while it is still morning
Come over to me, while your teeth still flash golden
Here in the hillside I have made your home
here, in my body, more loving than Donnan

    Bridei *crosses over to her*

Donnan: So you, my rival, Aslief of the mountain
 what good can you give instead of mine?
 We too, in Ireland, have your nature
 our tongue also is from your line
 What struggle we have is not with you
 Our enemies, believe me, are very real
 Our dual extinction is their only design
 but together we can resist their iron heel
Aslief: Rome calls you, Irishman, she's waiting now at Whitby
 There your light will be snuffed out
 Your scriptures, your places of learning
 burnt and destroyed, lost in a rout
 I see beyond your beehives and your chanting
 and your God, as you call him, will laugh out loud
 and I, Aslief of Ben Griam, will shout
 "This is what it costs to be so proud!"

> *Donnan, speechless and furious, defiantly and dramatically pulls his cloak around himself and exits. Aslief holds Bridei close and laughs.*

Aslief: See, Bridei, how he too fades into the hill
 Cnoc an Eireannaich holds his bed
 Smile on him, Bridei, your teeth like the sun
 For Donnan the long way has led
 his Celts to cross and subjugation
 but now in Strath Ulliean we hold his name
 although his faith is cold and dead
 It's gold, not Donnan, that flickers in history's flame

> *They exit. Music.*

Scene Four

*Two men, **Donald Mackay** (Seoras's father) and **Sandy Grant**, are fishing. They have a net which they repeatedly cast and haul in throughout. Behind them – or to one side – there is a table with five chairs, three of which are occupied by **Seoras**, **Catriona** and Seoras's mother **Meg**. On the table are bowls and spoons, set for a meal. The three have their heads bowed as if in prayer.*

Donald: The finny race are our tormentors
   Silver blue illusions
   they laugh at our brown sailed boats
   From ground to ground
   we find nothing, nothing, nothing
Sandy: I've traded my plough for endless fathoms
   my cattle for a yellowing net
   The voice of the ocean
   is a psalm to madness
   The mountains we see now are distant an cloudborne
Donald: Emptiness is a black dawning
   an futility a winter friend
   The Moray Firth is a salted desert
   Her song is of dorsal fin an gill
   her music is storm an drowning an gale
Sandy: Herring will buy me a green oil lamp
   Herring will fill the hungry barrel
   Herring will silt up the eye of the world
   but no herring we find from Burgh Head to Duncansby
   no herring a gull screech, a passing whale

   Meg rises from the table and calls to the men.

Meg: Come in, boys! The sky is darkening!
   The sea is gathering
   her wrinkled brow
   beyond where the sun can reach her!

   Come in, boys! There's young folk here!
   Back from across the world!
   Come back to bring you fresh welcome!
   To bring you hope, a hand an a story!

   The men cease their working. Music stops.

Donald: Who is it then, that ye have til make so much noise about it?
Meg: Who else but Seoras and Catriona? Back from New Zealand just like their letter said. Fresh off the coach no more than an hour.
Sandy: (*to **Donald***) Weel, is that no the thing, Donald? Yer own boy home til see ye!
Meg: Come now, the pair o ye.

*They cross the stage and enter the 'house'. **Seoras** and **Catriona** rise. **Catriona** embraces the two men warmly. **Seoras** and **Donald** shake hands rather stiffly to indicate the distance between them.*

Meg: Now is this no a fine thing?

Catriona: You're looking fine, Donald. An ye, Sandy, there's still that twinkle in yer eye.

Donald: It'll be from the cold. There's the Devil's nip in the air this day.

Meg: Then will ye all be seated, for there's porridge aplenty here til melt any cold.

Sandy: That'll be most welcome, Meg. I'll swear there's snow on the way.

***Meg** goes about the business of dishing out the food.*

Meg: Och you, you're always predicting snow. Even in July ye have us waiting for it.

Sandy: (*winking at **Catriona***) Ye can never be too careful.

Donald: I'm thinking it's over cold for snow, Sandy boy. Although a little fall would warm things up.

***Meg** dishes out the bowls.*

Meg: Here now, this is more like the thing.

The bowls are passed around, also a milk jug. Everyone awaits the Grace.

Donald: For what we are about to receive
may the Lord make us truly thankful.

Sandy: An God bless ye for yer brevity with the Grace, Donald Mackay.

Donald: Man, I could hear yer teeth chattering from here.

They all eat.

Meg: I just canna believe that ye're here, the pair o ye.

Sandy: It's a blessing from God, right enough, Meg.

Meg: That it surely is, Sandy.

Seoras: It was Catriona's doing. If it wasna for her we wouldna be here.

Meg: Is that so, now? Och but my, ye both look weel.

Catriona: It's the coming home that's done it. New Zealand's fine enough, but I missed the old place.

Seoras: Oh, so it's fine now, is it? It wasna that when we were out there.

Sandy: But ye've done weel enough, Seoras, that ye can return. No many can do that, none that I'll be knowing anyroad. Ach, the folk go right enough, but no many come back. No Seoras, ye've surely done weel.

Meg: Ay, that he has.

Donald: An what is it he's come back for, eh? Would anybody be telling me that?

Meg: Och, wheesht, man, an eat yer porridge. The loon's no a day back an ye have til be thundering at him.

Seoras: It's a fair question, Mother. Just a pity there's no more warmth attached til it.

Donald: Warmth, is it? An how much warmth is it that Sandy an mysel have in that ould boat we chase the fish in, eh? If we both live til be a hundred an fifty we'll still be paying it off.

Sandy: That's a fact. It surely is. (*he blows on his porridge*)

Donald: Maybe he's come til lend a hand at the herring nets, eh Sandy?

Meg: That he has no, Donald Mackay! Now will ye stop yer growlings an try til make the pair o them a bit more welcome.

Catriona: I know what you say is true, Donald, but Seoras is no going til the fishing.

Sandy: Weel, there's a wisdom in that.

Donald: An what exactly is the purpose o yer visit, Seoras? Or is it just a holiday ye're having, like the Duke?

Meg: Fer goodness' sake, anybody would think ye werena pleased til see the loon?

Seoras: I'm til pan for gold, just as I was doing in New Zealand.

Donald: Gold, is it? I'd have thought ye'd have found enough o thon stuff already?

Sandy: Maybe he's found all the gold in New Zealand, Donald. Is that no the way o it, eh Seoras?

Meg: The pair o ye stop teasing the boy!

Catriona: It's because o what we learned in New Zealand that we've come back til try it here.

Seoras: The geological layout is much the same. There's the same quartz rock formation. I'm going til look anyway.

Donald: D'ye really expect til find gold around here?

Seoras: Like I say, I'm goin til look.

Meg: Ye find nothing in this world if ye dinna look.

Donald: Oh is that a fact now? An why is it Sandy an mysel have been looking this past month an a half for herring an so far havena found any?

Meg: Ach, ye're impossible.

Catriona: Is the fishing that bad, then?

Sandy: Ay, Catriona, it's bad. As bad as it's ever been.

Donald: An the less fish we catch the more we fall intil debt. The leeches suck at ye, an they wonder why we growl?

Sandy: An there's nothing else for it. It's either the sea or starvation.

Meg: There'll be nobody starving at Helmsdale! What nonsense ye speak!

Donald: An what are we til eat, woman? Heather? Or maybe we could eat some o they grouse an pheasant the gentry are so keen on shooting? Or a deer? Or even an ould ewe?

Meg: An what's wrong wi the food ye're eating now, may I ask?

Sandy: Nothing, Meg. Nothing at all. But they wouldna be missing the odd beastie.

Donald: Ay, that they wouldna. But if they catch ye it's the jail. Hell, boys, maybe it's the Duke himsel that we should be eating?

Catriona: (*laughing*) Seoras, yer father would make a bonny Maori.

Meg: What has it come til, Donald Mackay, that ye have til blaspheme like a heathen?

Seoras: Calm yersel, Mother. He's only joking.

Sandy: Och, I wouldna be so sure. All I know is that the factors *do* patrol the straths like warders in a jail.

Meg: An I thought better o ye, Sandy Grant!

Donald: He's only speaking the truth. It's as if they think it'll all disappear if they dinna keep watching it all the time.

Sandy: But if Seoras finds gold here, Meg, we'll be eating better than his lordship!

Meg: Weel, that would make a fine change.

Catriona: We're almost positive there's gold in Strath Ulliean. The rock formations, the lie o the land, they're almost identical til what we experienced in New Zealand.

Meg: New Zealand, och ye'll have til tell me all about it.

Seoras: It's a beautiful country, Mother, plenty o room an a chance for everybody.

Sandy: Plenty gone from here til there. An til Australia.

Donald: Ay, an til every other damned place ye care til mention! Everywhere except where they're supposed til be.

Meg: An where would that be, pray tell?

Donald: Here, on the land. The place that gave them birth.

Meg: An havena ye no just finished telling us that there's nothing here?

Catriona: Many folk have done weel over there, Donald. They value their freedom.

Donald: Freedom? What freedom is there in exile?

Meg: There's many that would leave tomorrow if they could afford the passage.

Catriona: But this is home, Meg, an now we're back in it.

Sandy: But ye'll have already made yer fortune, Seoras, eh?

Seoras: Hardly a fortune, Sandy.

Sandy: Ach, but I'll be thinking ye've got gold bars stacked in some New Zealand bank vault, eh boy?

Catriona: Chance would be a fine thing.

Sandy: But they say that the gold miners make a fortune every day.

Donald: Ay, the same as us rich fishermen, eh Sandy? The only gold we ever see is in the sunrise.

Seoras: There are a few that strike it lucky an do make a fortune. But for the majority all they can hope for is a steady living.

Meg: An what more could a body hope for?

Donald: Gold, I would be thinking, an lots o it. They tell me it's like a fever. Is that no so?

Seoras: Ay, it can grip a man, but it's like a mirror til poverty, an if folk can see a way out o it then they'll go for it with everything they've got.

Sandy: Ye can see how it could happen. But surely the disappointment must be terrible?

Catriona: Only for those who are too desperate, Sandy, an for them there's always the taverns and whisky shops. If ye rush, ye find nothing. The steady approach is the one which pays in the end.

Seoras: But in a rush it's difficult no til be stampeded like all the rest.

Meg: An if ye find gold in the strath will we be overrun with folk?

Seoras: No if ye go about it the right way, Mother.

Donald: I'll be thinking that if ye do come across gold, or even an everfilling meal kist, that folk'll get til hear o it. Even if ye want them til or no.

Sandy: Ay, there's little that passes this way that doesna get a good telling.

Meg: Folk put too much store into gossip an lookin intil other folks' affairs!

Donald: It's only because a certain set o other folk concern themselves over much with our business. If we had control over our own affairs then we might no be so frightened aboot who gets off the mail coach.

Sandy: Soon it'll be the train. I was reading about it in the paper

Meg: Och the train'll never get past Golspie. A train til Helmsdale? Ye dinna want til believe everything ye read in that paper, Sandy Grant. Half o it's pure havers. Now if ye've all finished I'll take yer bowls.

> ***Meg*** *and **Catriona** stand up and the bowls are gathered in. They take them to the back of the stage.* ***Donald*** *and **Sandy** light up their pipes.*

Donald: Trains or no trains, what I'm saying is that folk will find out.

Seoras: It doesna matter if they do or if they dinna. The first thing we hev til do is find the stuff.

Donald: Ay, an that'll be the day.

Sandy: If ye're thinking o working up the Strath ye'll have til get the permission o the Duke's man.

Catriona: It seems strange that we have til ask him so that we can work in our own river.

Sandy: But that's it, Catriona. It's his river now.

Donald: Ay, an he'll be wanting the dog's share o anything that comes out o it. Whether it be gold, fish, or a pair o my ould socks!

Meg: (*coming back to the table*) An what exactly would yer socks be doing in the river, Donald Mackay?

Seoras: I'll have a word with the factor tomorrow. Who is it these days?

Sandy: Who else but Peacock? Ye'll find him strutting down around Dunrobin.

Catriona: (*she too returns to the table*) D'ye think he'll give us permission?

Sandy: Oh, ay. I'm sure he will. He canna really stop ye. But ye'd be wise no til tell him over much. In fact I wouldna be telling him anything at all.

Donald: Ye're alright there, Sandy boy. Tell the beggar nothing. That way he canna take anything off ye.

Meg: Ye're always thinking the worst o Mister Peacock.

Donald: An I've every damned right! If the man was like Jesus an could walk on the water he'd be out clearing us off the sea, as sure as fate.

Meg: He would do no such thing! An anyway, his wife's very nice.

Donald: It's no his wife who would implement the warrants.

    Meg returns to sink/backstage.

Seoras: But if it proves of benefit, now that things are bad, what is the harm in that?

Donald: A factor sees the world in a different way, Seoras, an that power they hold over us. It sends us out to the sea every morning on the tide.

Sandy: Ay, there's more than your hand on the tiller, Donald, that's for sure. (*pause*) Tell me, Seoras, what sort o gear d'ye need for this gold-digging business?

Seoras: Hardly anything at all. That's the beauty of it. A pick, a shovel, a pan. An that's ye kitted out.

Sandy: My goodness now, is that all there is til it?

Catriona: Ye can rig up some sluice gates if ye're on a good paying stretch. That way ye can maximise the flow o the river.

Sandy: Weel, weel. It all sounds pretty straightforward.

Donald: Dinna tell me ye're going til become a gold digger too, Sandy Grant?

Sandy: Ye canna blame a man for being interested now.

Seoras: But ye're right, Sandy, it is pretty straightforward. But it's here in yer head that ye have til be adept. For every pan ye wash something will be learned. The different gravels. The colour o the stones in the water. All these things have til be remembered.

Catriona: Seoras has a gift for it.

Seoras: Like I say, it's just a question of remembering; o knowing what ye're looking for, an what ye're looking at. If ye like, Sandy, I'll show you how it's done.

Sandy: Weel now, that's very good o ye, but we're off til the sea at first light on the tide. But we'll be back in a day or two an maybe then ye'll have found so much gold they'll have til carry ye around in a cart!

Donald: Then gold an Manson's whisky have the same effect.

Catriona: I feel ye've both got a lot til learn about gold digging.

Meg: (*returning to table*) Weel, I'm sure we wish ye well, the pair o ye. (*after a pause, sadly*) It seems now we've become a race o hunters, an I canna say I like the way o it. But in this life ye never get what ye want, or so it seems.

Donald: It's the getting o what we need that's denied us. Well, Seoras, I hope yer gold is no like the herring. For God alone knows where they've gone til.

Meg: Ach, ye no doubt stick yer big ugly plate over the side o the boat an scare them off!

Donald: Weel, there's many an ugly man on this coast is all I'm saying.

He puts his pipe away. **Meg**, **Catriona** *and* **Sandy** *carry the table to the back of the stage. As* **Seoras** *moves to help them,* **Donald** *grabs his wrist.*

Donald: Til see ye here, loon, does this ould man good. There are many in this village whose sons are gone from them. Distance does what death used til do.

Seoras: I'm glad til be here, father.

Donald: Yer mither aye tells me I drove ye away, an the good Lord knows my tongue hasna grown smoother with the years. But we're at the end o oor tethers here. Men go oot further. More often. Oor ranks thin, an I'm gettin too ould, an that disna help.

Seoras: What need ye o the fishing now, Father? Can ye no sell yer share in the boat over til a younger crew? I have money enough til ensure yer comfort.

Donald: Na, Seoras, I dinna want charity. A man must work an keep his head held high. But what greater pleasure would it give a father til see his son following on behind him? I was hard on ye in the past, but...

Seoras: (*as if convincing himself*) I left til find something in the world.

Donald: But ye can find it here. This is yer home.

Seoras: I've gone a different way from ye. It's too late til change that.

Donald: Change? Ye hevna changed. I aye thought ye were too good for here.

Seoras: Why must ye say that? I want more than nothing, I...

Donald: Is that what we are til ye? Nothing?

Seoras: Ye're my family.

Donald: Ay, an little stock ye seem til put in that.

Seoras: D'ye think it's been easy for me? I know the smell o hardship as weel as ye.

Donald: What hardship is there working for yer people here, now?

Seoras: (*softly*) We'll see.

Donald: Ay, we'll see.

Enter **Sandy**, **Catriona** *and* **Meg**.

Donald: Now come on, Sandy boy, we've nets til mend an sails til hang.

Sandy *puts his pipe away.* **Donald** *rises.*

Sandy: Ay, that we have. We'll no doubt be talking til the pair o ye later. By the Lord, it's fine til see some young folk coming back.

Donald: Ay, that it is. Even if it is til dig for gold. An the land here is just crying out for cultivation.

We'll bid ye all a good day. (*muttering*) Gold be damned.

Exit Donald and Sandy.

Meg: Ye'll excuse yer father, Seoras, but things are pretty low at the fishing now. They've been this way for some time. He gets a bit weary o it, as we all do.

Catriona: It's no life for men like them.

Meg: Ye know, when we first came here we had never even seen the sea afore.

Seoras: I know. Many drowned learning o it.

Meg: All his three brothers. An my youngest too. She's a hungry teacher, the sea.

Catriona: What do men have til hunt the sea for when there's wealth an plenty on shore? Meg, our strath, if we're fortunate, will give us all the life we need.

Seoras: Catriona, we dinna know that for sure. Granted it looks good, but we canna bank on it.

Meg: What need have we o banks in Helmsdale? Ye go intil Strath Ulliean, the pair o ye. Ye're young. Ye're clever. Ye're honest. She'll give ye all ye want. Ye'll see.

Music. Meg, Seoras and Catriona move forward from the table.

Catriona: When the sun beats down
onto the soft hillsides from the sky
there were my people
my mother, my father
when the sun beats down
they will be there in their number
in Strath Ulliean
in the Strath of Gold
when the sun beats down
onto the soft hillsides from the sky

Seoras: They took us to coastlands
bereft of all shelter
in pre-built houses
if you were lucky
They took us to coastlands
not ready for humans
there was neither drainage
nor topsoil there
they took us to coastlands
bereft of all shelter

Catriona: An we dreamed of safety an shelter
where the wind did not cut
where the sea drew no anger

deep in the straths of burn an river
in the knowing of placenames
in the attending to the dead
our days full of worry an terror
an we dreamed of safety an shelter
where the wind did not cut.

> *During the beginning of Catriona's speech* **Aslief** *has entered;*
> *and as* **Meg** *speaks, it's as if* **Aslief** *prompts her or calls her out.*

Meg: My tongue is the tongue of a lion
I will grow dark in the night wind
I will be there when next you look
in the place where you did not expect me
My tongue is the tongue of a lion
It sleeps beneath the hillsides
it sleeps beneath the skin
It is the weather of our predictions
My tongue is the tongue of a lion
I will grow dark in the night wind

Catriona: Salt dries our mouths, our fingers
It covers our bodies, is a silver curse
We were housed in the billets of an aristocrat's intention
Salt dries our mouths, our fingers
It turns our sodden bellies sour
it turns our hair to sticks
Our eyes become as jellyfish
Salt dries our mouths, our fingers
It covers our bodies, is a silver curse

> *Exit* **Meg**, **Seoras** *and* **Catriona**. **Aslief** *remains on stage.*
> *Music.*

Scene Five

*Music continues. **Aslief** stands to one side of the stage. Enter **Seoras** with pick, spade and pan. He begins to work. **Aslief** sings. **Seoras** does not hear her.*

Aslief: Your father's wise
O he is strong.
He ploughs the waves
O he reaps the sun.
His leaden heart
upon the ocean
O Strath Ulliean
O golden.

Those who seek an those who take
they to death
their way do make
Greed's shadow
their companion
O Strath Ulliean
O golden.

Seoras Mackay
the world is large
to the four winds
we do discharge
our hopes an dreams
our names we carve
O Strath Ulliean
O golden.

*Music stops. **Aslief** moves over to **Seoras** and observes him curiously for a moment. **Seoras** appears to be physically tired. His motions are weary and heavy.*

Aslief: Alone this morning are we?

***Seoras** almost drops his pan in surprise.*

Seoras: No more, it would appear.

***Aslief** moves around him, looking him up and down. She hums her tune. **Seoras** gets rather annoyed at this.*

Seoras: Where on earth did ye spring from?

***Aslief** ignores his question.*

Aslief: Catriona back in the village then? A little harmony lost there since ye came home, eh?

Seoras: Who are ye til ask such questions?

Aslief: (*wistfully*) Oh, nobody.

***Seoras** picks up his pan and continues his work. **Aslief** creeps up on him again and again he literally jumps.*

Aslief: There's gold enough in there for ye, Seoras Mackay.

Seoras: Look, what are ye doing here? I mean, are ye no far too old til be out this far from Helmsdale on yer own?

Aslief: Helmsdale is a shut eye til me. My place is til the north.

Seoras: (*laughing cynically*) Then ye work for the Duke, for no a soul lives there now. The coast holds Strath Ulliean's folk.

Aslief: Ay, that's true, very true. As til the Duke, he canna harm me.

Seoras: (*humouring her*) Then ye escaped the torches. Old woman, I salute ye! For ye're the only one.

Aslief: Yer wit almost suits ye, gold digger. But forget about me. Where I come from doesna concern ye, although ye are looking for me.

Seoras: (*irritated*) Yer mystery makes ye ridiculous. Watch out ye dinna fall down an drown in a bog.

A pause. His mood changes. He puts down his pan.

Forgive me, but this work is endless.

Aslief: Ay, drudgery loosens an fouls many a tongue.

Seoras *moves towards her and ushers her to sit down.*

Seoras: Won't you sit down, please? Ye must be tired. (*he produces a bundle of cloth from inside his shirt*) I have a bannag here. It was baked yesterday. It's all I've got left I'm afraid, but I'll gladly half it with ye.

Aslief: That would be fine. Ye always were a kind boy, Seoras.

Seoras: (*watching her eat*) Ye know me, or so it seems, but ye I canna seem til remember.

Aslief: My name is Aslief. I live on Ben Griam.

Seoras: I went there once. Poaching. There was three of us. We didna see any cottages.

Aslief: Then ye'll have til look a bit harder if ye want til find gold in Strath Ulliean.

Seoras: (*indignantly*) I know how til look for gold!

Aslief: It's not enough til know. Gold is an offering. An no everybody is offered. A man has til move mountains just til find a few grains. Be it o truth, o light, or be it o gold. But she waits for ye.

Seoras: A man who learns as he goes along, who remembers, he can find her. That's a scientific fact.

Aslief: Ah, science. (*she smiles*) No everybody can see. But I see, Seoras. I see.

Seoras: Then ye know o the metal? Ye know where she's til be found?

Aslief: She's in all the burns in all the straths.

Seoras: Is she here?

Aslief: Ye know fine she is.

Seoras: (*half-joking*) Is such knowledge kept on Ben Griam?

Aslief: It's kept by the wind. By the burns an rivers. It sleeps beneath the hill.

Seoras: Ye're a teller o legends then?

Aslief: (*rises*) I am Aslief o Ben Griam. I hear many musics.

Seoras: (*puzzled*) Ye remind me o someone. Are ye related til...

Aslief: (*cutting him off*) Catriona will be here shortly. Ye'll feel less confused an more at ease then.

Seoras: (*rising*) Forgive me for saying this, Mistress, but yer knowledge doesna please me. For how did ye acquire it? I've only just made yer acquaintance, but my name, an that o my wife, ye know. An as til *yer* name, I've heard no one speak it.

Aslief: (*laughing softly*) Oh, they speak it for sure. But only that they dinna recognise me in their conversation. Each time they speak o change, it is I, Aslief, o whom they speak. Each time they discuss fortune, it is I, Aslief. I sit on their tongues like religion. When ye speak o gold, it is I, Aslief, I who have given ye the desire!

Seoras: Desire? But...

Aslief: Ay, desire! The tears o Broath! The teeth o Bridei! Oh Seoras Mackay, what is gold til ye?

Seoras: (*uncertainly*) Surely it is wages... I mean, money for my wife, for our future, bairns some day. What else? I...

Aslief: (*seeming physically to grow in stature*) What else indeed? Inside ye, Seoras Mackay, there beats an honest enough heart. But as in all men behind that there lies want beyond reason, an hunger beyond meaning. This land ye dig has been yer people's since time an I were young. But where will ye stop, Seoras Mackay, til find gold? What will ye no do til acquire it? Look deep intil yer heart an tell me!

Seoras: (*not really understanding*) I hevna even found the slightest sliver, although the traces were promising a bit further down the burn. (*indignant and trying to cover up the fact that he is slightly frightened*) Look, I work hard!

Aslief: Hard work is the solo from a chorus. No everyone who follows ye here will wish til sing in that fashion.

Music starts softly.

Aslief: Look, Seoras, through this strath walk Hunger an Want!

*Two grey figures slowly cross stage. **Seoras** stares at them in disbelief and fear. Music continues under Aslief's speech.*

Aslief: They push at folk an break their will. They rob ye o her name an cry ye Legion. They will turn yer young hope til an old hatred. An yer kind heart intil a cruel bird that can pick the eyes out o life!

***Hunger** and **Want** exit. **Seoras** tries to speak but cannot say anything. His mouth hangs open. The music fades.*

Aslief: (*kindly*) Ye have come from Aotearoa, the land o the long white cloud. There ye did well.

Seoras: My eyes play tricks on me. I...

Aslief: Ye see what ye see. Remember the gold, Seoras, she's waiting on ye.

Seoras: These spectres... The faces o hell's own children, I...

Aslief: No spirit beings they. No, Seoras Mackay, they are o human manufacture. They are both warning and result. Where they lead, love can never follow.

Seoras: Then where do they go?

Aslief: Oh they will seek any destination. It could be yer soul, Seoras. As til their origins, the doors o that place can swing open in yer heart as sure as they swing open at Dunrobin.

Seoras: If we work the land, we can…

Aslief: The earth moves through the heavens. This land is but a ship.

Seoras: This ship belongs til the Duke.

Aslief: A temporary captain. A ghost upon the deck.

Seoras: His like have walked your deck long years now.

Aslief: What are years til Aslief o Ben Griam?

> *Seoras gets to his feet and shakes off what he has just experienced like a dog with a wet back.*

Seoras: Should I be lucky here I plan til go til the Duke an get him til implement some sort of licence system.

Aslief: The Duke has the flames o florins flickering in his eyes. In yer pan, Seoras, there flickers another kind o fire. See!

> *Aslief points to the pan and indicates that Seoras should pick it up. He does so. She begins to hum her tune again. Seoras takes on an expression of great surprise. He begins to swirl the water out of his pan excitedly.*

Seoras: In the name o…! Would ye credit that? I knew those traces were til be trusted! Yes, yes, there it is! Oh, Catriona will never believe this!

Aslief: She will, for there she is now at the turn in the burn. Ye can show her for yersel.

> *Seoras picks up a small nugget and drops the pan to the ground.*

Seoras: Ye, ye Aslief, ye put this here!

Aslief: The teeth an tears o the ages. Ye hold it in yer hand. Here now, wave til yer loved one.

> *Without thinking, automatically, Seoras waves with the hand that holds the nugget.*

Aslief: She'll have food an drink for ye. But now ye have the promise o food an drink for all.

Seoras: (*almost in a babble*) Gold! Gold! Catriona, gold! I've found gold! It's here right enough! Gold! Gold! (*he is almost dancing*) Gold! Gold!

Aslief: Let the joy have its moment, Seoras, but Hunger and Want are sour shadows. Their length is as long as human kind. Be warned, o Seoras Mackay, without respect an joy for her Strath Ulliean will become a desert til those who misuse her.

> *Exit Aslief. Seoras was not listening. Enter Catriona carrying a basket. He embraces her wildly.*

Seoras: Oh Catriona, it's gold, good quality gold, an there's much more
o it if I'm no mistaken. See! See! See!

He presses the nugget into her hand.

Catriona: Seoras, steady yersel. Ye're like a wee boy!

Seoras: But it was nothing til do with me. It was Aslief here, she ...

*He turns to where Aslief had been standing, then rushes across
the stage*

But she canna have gone! No far anyroads. She's an ould woman,
she ... she *was* here! I swear it.

Catriona: Take yer ease, Seoras, there's no-one here. I saw ye a good
hundred yards back an ye were on yer own, I'll swear til it. It's the
excitement o yer find. Come, sit down an have some food. Ye sound
like ye need it. (*he does so rather sheepishly*) I should never have left
ye out here on yer own. This place is ower big for one person til
work in. The mind can drift.

Seoras: (*deflated*) But this nugget is real enough.

Catriona: (*examining it*) Ooh, it's beautiful. But it looks nothing like
any other gold we've found.

Seoras: (*reviving a little*) Dinna worry, it's gold alright. Oh, Catriona, ye
were right, ye were *so* right. If ye rub it with a stone, see how it
shines!

*He rubs the nugget with a small stone. They both look at it
admiringly.*

Seoras: (*remembering*) But the old woman, Aslief, where ...?

Catriona: There's no one here save for ye an me. Look (*she indicates
around her*) the strath's empty. Believe yer eyes.

Seoras: I believe this metal, Catriona, an right now that's all I'm going
til believe. (*pause*) That woman *was* here. I spoke til her. Ye hev til
believe me. (*he takes the nugget*) She told me o this. This is hers.

Catriona: (*firmly*) It's yours. Ye found it. Ye. Nobody else. It's for yer
benefit an for the benefit o us all. That's why we're here, remember?
That's why more will follow us.

Seoras: She said Hunger an Want walk in this strath. An I saw them.
Grey an terrible they were. (*he shivers*)

Catriona: Of course they are. But in your hands is a way til defeat them.
(*she takes hold of the nugget*) This'll put hope back intil the folk.
Human voices can fill Strath Ulliean once again. Oh Seoras, maybe
now we really can come home!

She hugs him.

Seoras: Maybe so, maybe so.

They break.

Catriona: (*crossing stage*) Dinna doubt it, Seoras. For there's wealth in
this burn (*pointing*) an that one.

Seoras: But we dinna own them, Catriona, we can pretend that we do, but we dinna.

Catriona: But ye've found gold, real physical gold, here! (*pause*) Seoras, what is it that troubles ye?

Seoras: Ach, I'm no sure. In New Zealand it was different. The land was open an young an nobody owned it, no really. Ye could feel a sense o balance there. But here, ach, the scales are weighted against ye.

Catriona: So what are ye saying? That we should give up? But we've only just started!

Seoras: We'll no give up. The potential's here an we must explore it. There's nothing going til stop me doing that. But why all this doubt? We can achieve a balance if we tell the truth.

> *Seoras takes Catriona's arm and points to the horizon.*

Seoras: See that horizon, Catriona, over that an down the strath lies Helmsdale. A village full o hungry folk. An they'll come up over that horizon, och no from what ye or I may say, but from what they tell themsels. An they'll be wanting something, something they need so badly. Something, maybe, more than gold.

Catriona: I know. But we must secure what's ours.

Seoras: Hunger an Want, from what I can see, have no smiling happy faces. Desperation pushes them. They're no Maoris, Catriona, they're our own folk. They want their freedom more than they know.

Catriona: Then let them take it. For who's til stop them? No ye, no me.

Seoras: No but it's no up til us. Just think on a bit. Who in their right mind would sail the seas til make a living when there's wealth enough here, right under our feet, here on land? Ye said so yersel.

Our grandparents lived an died no far from here. It wasna them that let desolation loose in this strath. They had no tryst with Hunger and Want. But this time we canna let it go. This time we willna lose. (*he turns to Catriona*) Gold! Oh Catriona, we've found gold!

> *Music.*

End of Act I

Act II

"A stony view..."

Scene One

The scene is that of the goldrush village of Baile an Or – the Town of Gold. There is a crude tent: a blanket over a rope suspended over two poles and kept in place with rocks. There are shovels, spades, picks, pans, billy-cans etc. Music is heard. Enter Aslief.

Aslief: All seek gold
for life an love
a dream-filled death
a glimpse o heaven
all seek gold
she will not know them
O Strath Ulliean
O golden

Along the burns
the people pan
picking away their hopes
woman an man
score upon score
an still they come
O Strath Ulliean
O golden

Exit Aslief. Enter Seoras and Sandy. The music fades.

Sandy: Weel Seoras, ye must be fair pleased? There's over two hundred folk on the hill this morning. There's talk o a party arriving from Wick!

Seoras: (*he is troubled, but forces a wry smile*) Wick, eh? Weel I canna say I blame them for leaving thon place. I wish them luck.

Sandy: An they'll be needing it. So far ye're the only one I know that's found any gold. Which is why ye an me are partners!

Seoras: Weel, I hope ye dinna live til regret it. But just look at them, Sandy! (*indicating offstage*) Down there at the burn's bank. Picking an digging an shovelling! Throwing away whatever pay dirt there is! No sooner does one find what he thinks is gold than he's surrounded like a dead sheep by crows. It's hopeless!

Sandy: But it's no hopeless! Ye know there's gold there! It's the fishing that's hopeless! That's why all these folk are here. Ye've given them hope, when all they had afore them was starvation an the poor-hoose. An there's nothing in the parish save for what goes intil the graveyard.

Seoras: But I'm no charity, damn it! If we could only get some organisation here. Some order. Some system. Then honest men might have a chance. It's January an the frosts are heavy. I fear for the poor souls. Some may die. Then what?

Sandy: Most o these men are fishermen. Ye'd be surprised what they can endure.

Seoras: But this isna what I wanted! No this mad scramble! We're losing more than we can ever find this way.

Sandy: The seas are empty, Seoras. Yer gold discovery came along like a Godsend. A miracle some say.

Seoras: Then I wish I'd never found it! For this is no miracle, this is madness!

Sandy: But have ye no talked til Peacock, the factor? Did he no have anything til say? What about the Duke himsel?

Seoras: Ach, the Duke! He's 'indisposed' at the present. Abroad, Peacock says. It'll take time for him til catch up on these goings-on. Then Peacock can just sit an watch which way the wind blows an see how much the estate can make. But if this cold spell doesna end we'll discover nothing here but misery.

Sandy: As if we havna had oor share o that. These folk, most o them anyway, walk the ten mile from Helmsdale every day, an the same ten mile back at night.

Seoras: Exactly. If we were sensible we could provide shelter for them here. Cabins, proper tents.

Sandy: Och, they'll no stay here at night. Did ye no know the place is haunted?

Seoras: Haunted?

Sandy: (*pointing*) Ay, that hill's no called Cnoc na Beiste for nothing. The Hill o the Monster, Seoras. (**Seoras** *laughs more out of tiredness than humour*) Ye can laugh at it now, but at night, up here in a tent, it's a different matter. Strange things have been seen in this part o Strath Ulliean.

Seoras: Well, nothing could be stranger than this lunacy! This morning two men woke up an found their boots frozen ontil their feet!

Sandy: Dinna be getting so agitated, bouyag! Things'll sort themsels out. In a few days, maybe a week, a month even, a lot o folk will have gone home. Ye can talk til those left then. Explain what's best for them til do. They'll listen. Ye'll see.

Seoras: I suppose ye're right, Sandy. There's no much else for it the now. (*thoughtfully*) Or is there, I wonder?

Sandy: What d'ye mean? The folk are fevered. Ye said so yersel.

Seoras: But that's it exactly. The folk'll aye be fevered. It's experienced hands we need here. I'll write til Otago an get Cameron an MacKenzie til try their luck here in Strath Ulliean. What they've learned in New Zealand we need here. Maybe, if I tell them straight o their prospects, they'll bring others. I'll have til write til Peacock again. There are a few schemes I can put til him. He's got til be made til see the potential here. He's got til!

Sandy: Seoras, this gold, if it's here, is for our people. It's theirs by right an by need. If ye bring in professionals, foreigners, there'll be trouble. The folk willna stand for it!

Seoras: Then we might as weel stop now! Can ye no see? It's steady, experienced diggers we need here. Just look around ye at the way the sides o the burns've been cut away. If this carries on how long afore the Sutherland estate joins with his neighbour, the Duke o Portland, an keeps us off with guns?

Sandy: Portland's weel known til be daft, ye canna...

Seoras: (*cutting him off*) Sandy, the sporting fraternity have no love for us! They dinna want any gold diggers on this hill. They cleared the strath for their sheep once afore, mind? If we dinna come up with results by the summer we'll be denied access til the diggings. An what'll the folk do then? It's the only way.

Sandy: Maybe so, maybe so. But they trust ye, Seoras. Ye're one o them. They'll feel ye've betrayed them.

Seoras: I'm trying til help them! Unless the herring jump out o the sea tell me another way?

Sandy: (*after consideration*) Ye're a good lad, Seoras, an I'll stand by ye. They might listen. They might no.

Seoras: The only alternative is ruin, an that I canna afford. I've been around the world an back, an I thought, I thought I'd left this fever in New Zealand. But I'd forgotten poverty. I'd forgotten the noise o it. I'd forgotten its speed. Only the rich are quiet. Only the well-fed are slow. It's balance, balance we need, balance. (*pause*) Ach, Sandy, maybe it would have been better if I'd stayed in Otago?

Sandy: What kind o talk is this? We need ye here. An we're glad on it. If all this comes til nothing, if the Duke kicks us off, or even if there's no gold nor anything else, it's better that we tried. At least here we can leave our mark behind. On the sea ye leave nothing, no even a space ahind ye. Ye just disappear. I'd rather be here than any other place in the world. I knew it the first time I heard ye speak o it. Strath Ulliean, she's home til me.

Seoras: (*happier*) Then we've got work til do, Sandy Grant, (*he picks up a shovel and hands it to* **Sandy**) for there's plenty o gravel here needin panned.

Sandy: (*feeling his back*) Man, I feel as though I've dug doon til New Zealand already.

Seoras: Then we'll have til dig right back up! C'mon, Sandy, for I'm feeling lucky.

> **Seoras** *picks up his pan and a pick. Both men exit. Music rises. Enter, rather furtively,* **Peter Dominicus Sinclair**, *a jeweller. He is dressed in fashionable, but garish, Victorian knickerbockers. He has a lens which hangs around his neck and through which he peers at stones and other small rocks. He gives off the air of a Scrooge, or a miser, yet somehow generous in his vocabulary.*

*When he speaks, it is with the perfect English of the Invernessian.
He carries a carpet-bag.*

Sinclair: Let me present myself. Before you stands Peter Dominicus
Sinclair, esquire, of Inverness, only four doors from the railway
station. Jeweller and Goldsmith to the Court of Her Majesty. But you
can call me Peedee. Everybody else does. I'm very well known. All
my stock is engraved with traditional Highland patterns and at
moderate prices. (*he takes out his elaborate pocket watch*) I guarantee
all my watches for two years! I mean, you can't beat that, can you?
And what am I doing here in Strath Ulliean, I hear you ask? Well, if
you'll bear with me I'll explain. In all richly auriferous countries the
rocks which originally contain the gold that is collected by the digger
or miner, belong to what geologists classify as the lower silurian
group, consisting of various sub-crystalline metamorphic schists, of
which gneiss and mica slate are familiar types. These schists are
frequently penetrated by veins of quartz, which, from their size and
form, are often designated by the gold miners "reefs" or "quartzites".
In these reefs gold originally occurs; and when the schists and
quartzites in question are disintegrated by ice or other actions the
contained gold is to be looked for in their debris. Got that? Good. It's
just so that you know.

And that's what they're doing here. Looking for gold in the debris.
And they do find it, you know. Some three hundred and fifty pounds
in weight so far. To the value of twenty thousand pounds sterling, as
far as I can gather. And to gather it in is my duty – as a jeweller.
Enterprise takes one to many seemingly barren shores. Initiative, my
dear friends, is like Pinocchio's nose. Mmm. (*he absent-mindedly
rubs his nose*) I shall set up a stall in this rather ramshackle
encampment. A good digger will always recognise an honest set of
scales. And after all, I have *real* money! And that's what folk are after
these days, real money! These tents are no more than blankets and
poles. I can be of some service here, I think, both to these diggers
and to myself. Ladies and gentlemen, profit is a large word. Sweeter
than the morning dew. Peedee Sinclair, I'm sure you'll agree, is no
ordinary jeweller. Friends I bid *adieu*. I'll be back presently.

*He exits. Music rises again over following. Enter **Meg** and
Catriona carrying a large kist.*

Meg: My man sleeps now
in the sea's green mouth
out past Noss Head
to a dream

My man sleeps now
on a bed of rock
on a bed of surf
the firth his prayer

Catriona: The storm rose like Leviathan
    in a black anger
    the boats like sheep
    running to the fank

    The masts like matches broken
    the sails blown to rags
    an the men entangled
    in death's salt wrappings

> *Music changes to the theme of Aslief's song. Enter **Aslief**.*
> ***Catriona** and **Meg** freeze.*

Aslief: The land will kiss
    the sea's green face
    it gives its soul
    to that briny place
    into its depth
    we pour our race
    O Strath Ulliean
    O golden

    The sun is red
    out in the west
    an ten dead men
    go to their rest
    our brave an strong
    our first an best
    O Strath Ulliean
    O golden

> *Music fades. Exit **Aslief**. Enter **Seoras** and **Sandy**. **Meg** crosses*
> *to **Seoras** and hugs him.*

Meg: Oh Seoras. *Ochone, ochone**.

Seoras: Mother, for goodness' sake, what's the matter.

> ***Meg** is unable to speak for weeping.*

Catriona: It's your father, Seoras. He's been drowned.

Seoras: But, how...?

Catriona: His boat, an the Boy John. They were caught in a squall. It rose out of nowhere, seemingly. They didna stand a chance.

> *As the three figures stand in silent shock, **Sandy** flies into a guilt-ridden rage.*

Sandy: I knew it! I telt him no til go oot without me. Til wait. No til go oot shorthanded. Damn the man an his stubbornness! Damn! Damn!

Meg: (*recovering slightly*) Dinna be blaming yersel now, Sandy. It's no yer fault. He kent the sea as weel as ye. He kent what he was doing. He had til go oot, an that's all there was til it. Ye know that.

---

*Sorrow, sorrow

Meg crosses to *Sandy*.

Meg: Be glad ye were spared.

Sandy: But...

Meg: No "but"s now.

Seoras: (*to Catriona*) It's ten long miles to Helmsdale. We'd better get back. We've til see til the funeral, the minister, the...

Meg: (*overhearing*) There'll be no need for that.

Catriona: (*to Seoras*) His body was never found, Seoras. None o them were. Let her rest awhile.

Sandy: (*muttering almost unintelligibly*) I should've been with him. I should've. I... I...

Meg: Why, man, ye're alive. God has saved ye. Be glad. Be glad.

Sandy: But Meg, I...

Meg: But nothing. Ye're right til be here. (*she looks around*) Oh but that more o ye were.

Sandy: (*trying to pull himself together*) There's more on that score every day, Meg. Some three hundred this morning.

Meg: Then pray til God there's three hundred more after them, an after them still more. (*she rises resigned*) Now Seoras, that brings me to the contents o this kist.

Seoras: What about it?

Meg: Just this. Inside it ye'll find a goodly supply o flour, tea, coffee, sugar, beef, bacon, soup, an other like incidentals that yer diggers can buy.

Seoras: Buy?

Catriona: That's right, Seoras. Yer mother plans til open up a shop here in Strath Ulliean. An since ye dinna seem til need me til work with ye I plan til help her.

Seoras: It's no that I dinna need ye, it's just...

Meg: (*interrupting*) I've been thinking it over for some time. An when I got the news o yer father, weel, that settled it. Besides, a shop might entice more folk til stay on. It'll give them the chance o comfort here on the hill rather than exhaust themselves over a twenty mile march every day.

Seoras: (*scratching his head*) It might at that.

Sandy: On that we'll see. But where are ye going til have such a shop, Meg? There's nothing here save for a thin collection o tents. An them no more than blankets.

Meg: I plan til rig up shelter in the lee o the gable end o the ould Ulliean kirk. My mother an father worshipped there in their day. The place'll be put til good use til Donald Mattheson arrives with the hut I've ordered from him. Sure, it'll be a long time since any soul was saved in this parish.

Sandy: A wooden shed, ye say? What if...

Meg: My goodness, man! Ye dinna expect me til sleep out in the open air at my age?

Seoras: Ye're certainly organised, I'll say that for ye. I wish more were like ye.

Meg: I've got Wullie Manson, the grocer, til supply an deliver the stores I'll need each week. There's never been so many folk buying in Helmsdale since the great days o the herring. They dinna cry him Mister Ten Percent for nothing.

Catriona: Think on it, Seoras, maybe a wee settlement could spring up here!

Sandy: Lord now, would ye imagine that?

Meg: The Lord works in mysterious ways, Sandy Grant. An he's given us Baile an Or. The Town of Gold!

Sandy: Baile an Or. Weel, weel.

Seoras: Now come on. Let's no get carried away! One hut doesna make a town, gold or otherwise. The estate has til come til some sort o decision about licensing. I'm waiting on a reply til my letters. An when we get it, that'll be the make or break o it.

Catriona: But it would be truly wonderful til have folk livin here again, Seoras, d'ye no think?

Seoras: It sounds good, that I'll admit.

Sandy: 'It sounds good'! Would ye listen til him? Boy, are ye no the canny one!

Meg: He's right til be canny. For canny men live a long life.

A silence falls. They remember the tragedy. **Seoras** *goes to* **Meg**.

Seoras: About Father, we must...

Meg: Dinna fret, Seoras. The Reverend Clark is coming up the morn's morn til have a remembrance service for all the men lost. He'll hev it in the ould kirk here, what's left of it anyway. (*pause*) That's what he'd like, believe me. (*she looks around her*) Maybe ye could get yer gold diggers til make up the congregation, no?

Seoras: (*with a gentle smile*) That I surely can.

He embraces her. They part.

Meg: Now come on, Sandy boy. Stop standin there gawking an take an end o this kist. I'll have til get it under cover afore the weather breaks.

Sandy: Ye're no proposing til carry it yersel?

Meg: (*as if she is talking to a child*) No. I'm proposing that we both carry it. Lord man, Catriona an mysel carried it all the way up the hill from the back o Manson's cart! I may be gettin on, but I'm no a cripple.

Sandy: (*lifting*) Weel, if ye think ye can manage?

Meg: Oh I do, I do.

They lift and move off.

Meg: I'll see ye two later. (*to* **Sandy**) Come on boy, I've seen a snail sleepwalk quicker!

Exit **Meg** *and* **Sandy**.

Seoras: (*softly*) She seems til have taken it weel. On the surface anyway.

Catriona: We all cope in different ways. But she's strong. She said she always knew he'd be lost. Something in his eyes. The pallor o his face. But she's no fisherman's widow, no yer mother. Which is why she thought o the shop. (*she sighs*) I must say, I feel a bit o a widow mysel these days.

Seoras: (*not really listening*) Oh?

Catriona: (*mocking him to hide her anger and concern*) Oh? Is that the best you can do? (*pause*) I never see ye. Ye're always up here with Sandy. At least in New Zealand we were together.

Seoras: This is no New Zealand.

Catriona: Ye're telling me! Is it no becoming for a woman til help her man here then?

Seoras: The conditions are different. It's ower cold an rough. There's hundreds o folk an...

Catriona: It was the same in Otago! But ye were a different man then. Ye were bright. Happy.

Seoras: (*he goes towards her*) I'm still the same man.

Catriona: Weel it's hard til believe. It's just... I dinna find yer absence easy. I'm no used til it. We used til be together all the time. A team.

Seoras: We're still a team. But like I say, it's different here. There's... ach, there's loads o things!

Catriona: What's wrong, Seoras? Are ye unsure? Does yer own success frighten ye? Ye always strove for success. What's wrong now that you have it?

Seoras: What questions are these? Look, we're a long way from success here. We have til organise an make it work. Somehow, I...

Catriona: Seoras, ye've found the gold, but ye have til learn til let it go. Ye canna do everything. Ye're only one man. Ye're no the Duke.

Seoras: Dinna I just know it!

Catriona: All I'm saying is that ye can only do so much.

Seoras: Stop going on about me! It's no me! I'm no important! It's the hundreds o men digging in the hill, an the hundreds more at the sea. What we have here is individual chaos. What we need is co-operation. These gold diggings must serve the community, no ruin it.

Catriona: Ruin has no place in this strath. No any more.

Seoras: Every day, when I work here, I see where the fields used til be. It's a cold sight. It can turn the heart to ice.

Catriona: There are many here whose hearts desire a flame. They'll join together behind ye!

Seoras: They might if the work would let them. All the daylight is spent digging. The nights are lost til sleep. (*pause*) Ach, I know I'm just one man an this whole thing's no my personal crusade, but remember our bargain? It was ye who thought it up. Ye wanted us til come here. Weel, we're here. Ye wanted us til dig for gold. We have, an much til my amazement we've found it. Take a look around ye, this is all yer work! Before ye stands yer creation!

Catriona: (*finding his whole tone faintly ridiculous*) Weel, I'm flattered ye think all this is my doing.

She moves across and caresses him.

Catriona: Oh Seoràs, what doubts an torments have found a home in your heart? Dinna ye love me any more? Is that it?

Seoras: Oh Catriona, I love ye fine enough. (*he kisses her*) An as til this damn strath, I love her too. Dinna ask me how or why or anything else. I just do. Under her skin is our freedom. I just feel it.

Catriona: An what now o New Zealand?

Seoras: (*laughs*) Let the Maoris have New Zealand. It's theirs anyway. Why travel the world til find what's right under yer nose?

Catriona: Then ye must follow yer nose. But never lose yer happiness, Seoras, for that's my happiness too, an once it's gone all the gold in Strath Ulliean canna buy it back.

Seoras: I know. But something has til happen. An it'll have til happen soon.

Catriona: It will. On that ye can rest assured. (*they part*) About yer father, Seoras. Ye dinna have til be so resolute for me. Let the tears come if ye wish them.

Seoras: (*coldly*) What good are tears now? He wouldna thank ye for them anyway.

Catriona: (*almost under her breath*) Why do we hold our feelings so close til oursels here, like secret stones or some black shame?

Seoras comes up behind her and spins her round.

Seoras: But, Catriona, we must work!

Catriona: (*laughing*) Ay then, let's work.

Seoras and Catriona exit arm in arm. Music (rises into Aslief's theme). Enter Aslief.

Aslief: Quiet is the tongue
of the river tonight
her golden voice
has frozen
The diggers rest
is a frozen home
O Strath Ulliean
O golden
The tents an huts
of Baile an Or
a ring
of shabby mushrooms
A shovel, a pick
a tin basin
O Strath Ulliean
O golden

Exit Aslief. The music into the next scene merges into a psalm.

Scene Two

The scene is still the gold rush town of Baile an Or. From offstage we hear the massed tones of a Gaelic psalm*. After it has died down, enter **Sandy**, **Seoras**, **Catriona** *and* **Meg**, *who is drying her eyes.*

Meg: Now was that no a lovely service? The Reverend Clark is a bonny speaker.

Sandy: That he is, Meg, that he is. If no a little on the windy side.

Catriona and Seoras sit quietly together.

Meg: Ach, ye're just a bad listener. But somehow the singing gives a body comfort.

Sandy: It surely does, an no a word o a lie on it. An can those diggers no sing?

Meg: It was right good o them til turn oot in such numbers.

Sandy: Donald was weel kent up an down the coast, Meg. I dinna think there'll be a pick swung in the hill the day.

Sandy goes over to Seoras and Catriona as Meg still dabs the hanky to her eyes.

Sandy: Dinna be ower glum now, bairns. We have til put things behind us. We canna undo what's been done. More's the pity on us. Yer father's at his rest an God bless him in that. (*he pulls a hip flask, rather slyly, out of his pocket*) Here, have some *uisge beatha*.† It'll cheer ye up a little. Go on now, (*he offers the flask*) an if ye're good I might sing ye my new song.

Seoras takes the flask and drinks.

Catriona: Yer song?

Sandy: Ay, it's about the gold diggings here in Strath Ullean. All the boys up the burn sing it.

Seoras: (*he hands flask to Catriona, who drinks*) Ye dinna mean til tell me ye're responsible for thon load o rubbish?

Sandy: It's no rubbish! (*to Catriona*) Would ye listen til him. He canna tell one end o a tune from the other.

Catriona: (*laughing and handing back flask*) I'd like til hear it, Sandy.

Sandy: (*to Seoras*) D'ye hear that now, ye great stirk? Yer wife at least has a taste in music.

Seoras: What ye do's no music.

---

*Psalm 73 verse 23: "Whom have I in heavens high but thee…" (Sung by Precentor Iain Murray and the church congregation of Dornoch, recorded by the BBC in 1951. Source: Columbia World Library of Folk and Primitive Music, compiled and edited by Alan Lomax. Vol VI, Columbia SL 209 – side 2; ML 4946)
†'water of life', ie whisky.

Sandy: (*to* **Meg**, *who has drifted off into a dwam*) I was just thinking o singing a wee song, Meg. Ye'll no mind? I'm sure himsel would enjoy it.

Meg: Ay, on ye go, Sandy boy. Ye're aye good at cheering a body up.

> **Sandy** *takes a swig from the flask and prepares for his song. Music accompanies him. His delivery is that of a hybrid between Harry Lauder and Will Fyffe-type music hall. He bows.*

Sandy: I'm off til Strath Ulliean
my fortune for til try
I'll be gone a month or so
so friends goodbye
til dig the precious metal
an sell it til the King
Oh digging gold, ye know
is a great an wondrous thing

Seoras: It's terrible!

Catriona: Shhh!

Sandy: (*unperturbed*) This is the chorus.

So I'll jog along the road
with a pick an a spade
with a dainty pair o brogues
newly made
a gallon o pure til cheer me on my way
I'm off til Strath Ulliean
at the dawning o the day

When I come back
with plenty gold til show
I'll buy a pub
for Sandy Grant an Co
I'll go til Inverness
an I'll buy the Maggot Green
for that's where all the bonnie lassies
can be seen

(*chorus*) So I'll jog along the road &c

I'll marry a little wifie
perhaps she may be here
just look at all the lassies
they're turning white with fear
but dinna fash now, lassies
some'll have til want
for ye canna all be
Mrs Sandy Grant

(*chorus*) So I'll jog along the road &c

> **Sandy** *finishes his song and is so pleased with himself that he has danced right across the stage and collided with* **Peacock**, *the*

factor, who has just entered. **Peacock** *is dressed as a factor usually is: tweed, boots etc.*

Peacock: (*looking straight into* **Sandy** *'s face*) A wee ceilidh, is it?

Sandy *backs off.*

Peacock: And here's me thinking I could hear a psalm from further down the burn?

Meg: And indeed ye did, Mister Peacock. We had a service for the men recently lost. Ye'll hev heard?

Peacock: That I have, Mrs Mackay. And let me pay my respects an express the great sympathy my wife and I feel for you in this your time of loss. Donald will be sorely missed.

Meg: Thank ye for yer kindness, Mister Peacock, an til Mrs Peacock. But we must bear up, for the sea, she's a hungry mistress.

Peacock: Indeed she is, Mrs Mackay, indeed she is. But it's good to see that you have so many family able to be with you at this unfortunate time.

Peacock *nods at* **Seoras** .

Seoras: Then ye got my letter?

Peacock: I have received more than one letter, Seoras.

Seoras: Then ye'll have relayed them til the Duke?

Catriona: Will the Duke be visiting the diggings, Mister Peacock?

Peacock: Unfortunately he will not. His Grace, at present, is in Egypt.

Sandy: Egypt? Dinna tell me he's after a monument like his father? Is one o they things no enough?

Meg: Sandy Grant, will ye no hold yer tongue?

Peacock: That's alright, Mrs Mackay. Sandy is well known for his, er, wit. If you must know, His Grace is on tour, and will not be back until the summer.

Seoras: The summer! But that's far too late! We need measures implemented now. In my letters I made that plain.

Peacock: Ah yes, your many letters. But I hear you've been writing about the prospects of Strath Ulliean to more than myself.

Catriona: The Royal Mail is open til everybody, Mister Peacock.

Peacock: (*ignoring her*) Let me tell you, Seoras, colonial miners will not be welcome on the Sutherland Estate.

Sandy: And why no? Access til the diggings is available til all who want til try it. What does it matter where they come from?

Peacock: They would be mercenaries, Sandy, surely you can see that?

Seoras: Then why have ye got six miners from South Africa sailing intil Leith next week, Mister Peacock?

Sandy: Ye canna deny it!

Peacock: (*thinking on his feet*) Rumour often runs ahead, while truth lags someplace behind, Sandy. (*to* **Seoras**) Their remit is purely one of surveillance, I assure you.

Seoras: An what d'ye think we're doing? We're surveying too!

Peacock: I am well aware of that, which is why I am here. I have to put to you the conditions under which the Sutherland Estate will tolerate any further diggings.

Seoras: Have ye no read my proposals?

Peacock: Your proposals are completely unacceptable!

Seoras: How d'ye know? Ye've never even tried them out! Ye know nothing about gold fields, Mister Peacock. I've worked in them for years.

Peacock: I know how to manage this estate, Missster (*he almost hisses the word*) Mackay! I've no doubts as to your qualifications in digging.

Seoras: Then why d'ye no implement my suggestions? In many gold fields in New Zealand and Australia these things are commonplace.

Peacock: With all due respect, this is not the Antipodes. Here we have many other interests to maintain.

Seoras: If it's just a question o money then money can be had *if* ye do as I suggest. It's almost guaranteed!

Sandy: But maybe it's no a question o money at all, eh Mister Peacock?

Peacock: That's a slanderous remark, Sandy Grant, and you may retract it!

Sandy: I will not!

Peacock: His Grace has acted most graciously and liberally towards the diggers on *his* estate.

Sandy: Would ye listen til him? 'His estate'. How can it be 'his' estate, him being a Sassanach? An his father afore him!

Peacock: I am not prepared to argue in public the hereditary nature of His Grace's affairs!

> *Sandy drinks from his flask with his back turned on the company.*

Meg: And neither are we, Mister Peacock. Pay no heed til Sandy. His latest song has made him a little light-headed, I'm thinking.

Peacock: No offence taken, I assure you, Mrs Mackay. Now, Seoras, on these matters it would be better if we gave ourselves some privacy.

Seoras: No, Mister Peacock, anything we discuss we discuss right here.

Catriona: Surely Mister Peacock has nothing til hide?

Peacock: Indeed I have not. (*he produces some papers*) I'm sure you'll find these regulations fair and fitting.

Seoras: As are mine.

Peacock: Your notions are pure fancy!

Seoras: They are no such thing! An ye'll hear them in front o witnesses. First, all claims til be given a section o river. Second, these workings should be at a minimum rent. Three, a diggers' register o rights an the appointment o a goldfield warden til guarantee said rights an til protect the diggers from unscrupulous dealers an conmen.

Sandy: There was one o them up here the other day. We'd all be eating sand at his rates.

Seoras: Exactly. Now finally, a guaranteed wage an food an clothing for all diggers who register claims.

Peacock: (*laughing*) It is totally unrealistic.

Seoras: It would ensure ye a regular workforce an a paying goldfield with a steady an healthy future.

Peacock: My God, man, what you propose is tantamount to trade unionism!

Catriona: Tut tut, we canna be having that now.

Seoras: It's proven practice, Mister Peacock.

Peacock: So ye say. But the Estate is not a benevolent society. All you cite are demands. How is the Estate going to gain from these gold diggings? Or is that a mere oversight?

Seoras: It's ye who have the oversight, Mister Peacock. The rents on yer Estate, as far as I can gather, are kept deliberately low. Ye rely too much on sheep. Ye could quite justifiably charge higher rents an increase yer income if ye made more land arable.

Peacock: (*aghast*) How dare you presume to tell me my own business!

Catriona: But ye will tell us ours.

Seoras: The Estate *will* benefit from the gold diggings, a blind man can see that. There's guaranteed earnings an greater spending power through the increase in the population. There's rent an accommodation. Ye could even charge a token fee for the licences if ye must. Even a one percent levy til the Estate on all gold sold. Ye could arrange that with the jewellers easy enough.

Peacock: But these are all tenuous earnings. Even invisible.

Sandy: What else is there for it! It's the herring that are invisible!

Seoras: The more gold diggers organised and working in Strath Ullean the greater the benefit til the Estate.

Peacock: But that's exactly my point. What if everybody wanted to be a gold digger? What about the crofting? The fishing? What about those who wish to shoot and flyfish in the area? How can they with these disruptions? There's nothing about any of these in your demands.

Seoras: They're *no* demands! They're reasonable proposals!

Catriona: The gold diggings'll be a seasonal thing for most folk, Mister Peacock. Afore the seed time, an after the harvest.

Sandy: Ay, an atween the herring seasons. If the herring ever come back, that is.

Meg: (*to Peacock*) If it wasna for the diggings many families would be hard up against it. Ye know how it is these days?

Peacock: (*his patience is beginning to go, as is his 'niceness'*) I know exactly how it is in these days! Seoras, no doubt your heart is in the right place. Idealism is natural in the young. But your head is in the clouds. Now, if you'll be so kind, I'll read to you the conditions and regulations drawn up by the Sutherland Estate.

Seoras: If ye must.

Sandy: I hope there's something in it about putting a roof on the ould kirk.

Meg: Ye're right there, Sandy. Folk shouldna be expected to worship under the open sky.

Peacock: (*sifts through his papers and reads*) The Sutherland Estate – Parish of Ulliean – re the Gold Mines licence by His Grace George Granville William, Duke and Earl of Sutherland, KG – to those hereafter known as the Miner, as stated April 6th, 1869.

Sandy: Is that it?

Meg: Will ye no shoosh an let the mannie speak!

Peacock: In consideration of the sum of one pound to be paid to the Duke and Earl by the Miner, this licence lasting the period of one calendar month and will thereafter terminate. This licence entitles the Miner to dig and search for gold in the alluvial deposit along the sides of the Ulliean, Suisgill and Torrish burns and nowhere else. Also the Miner shall, weekly, for the period of his licence, on a fixed day, make declaration in which he shall state the exact weight of gold obtained by him and he shall be ordered on behalf of the Crown to hand over to the acting Crown Agents one tenth part of all gold so obtained by him.

There are gasps and groans from those listening.

The miner shall have no right, under this licence, to erect any hut, tent, or any other building, on any ground in the district. Also the Miner shall protect his own claim and no warranty as regards it is hereby given to him. In the event of any Miner failing to fulfil the foregoing conditions the licence will be terminated and the Miner shall not be entitled to take up or enter upon any other claim.

He finishes reading and appears to be very pleased with himself.

There you are now. A finer set of regulations it would be hard to draw up. I have here a copy for you, Seoras, so that you can distribute it among the diggers.

*He tries to hand paper to **Seoras**, who strides past him in a rage.*

Seoras: I knew it, I knew it, I knew it!

Peacock: (*surprised*) Is there something wrong?

Seoras: Wrong? Peacock, d'ye know how many diggers there are on the hill at this very minute?

***Peacock** opens his mouth but nothing comes out.*

Catriona: Over five hundred, Mister Peacock.

Seoras: Ay, an d'ye know the average wage they earn?

Peacock: (*unsure of himself suddenly*) I can't quite quote you the figures, but I hear it's quite substantial.

Sandy: Five shillings a week, if ye're lucky. I'm saving up til go til Egypt too!

Seoras: After yer monthly rent o a pound ye willna be able til get til Helmsdale!

Peacock: Look, it's not a rent. It's a licence for a claim. That's what you yourself wanted, was it not?

Seoras: How can we afford a pound a month? Be reasonable.

Peacock: I am by nature a reasonable man, I assure you. But you know as well as I do that most miners never declare truly how much gold they find. Under the Crown Royalty we will be able to gauge more accurately how much gold is actually being discovered and proceed accordingly.

Sandy: Ye'll find a healthy disregard for yer Crown among most o the diggers here, I'm thinking.

Seoras: If ye implement these regulations, Mister Peacock, ye'll be denying the ordinary man access til try his hand. An him the one that actually needs it til survive!

Peacock: We must have regulation and order.

Seoras: Ay, but no this, this…

Catriona: This disaster. (*to Peacock*) Ye'll end the diggings afore they have a chance til really begin!

Peacock: The estate must extract a suitable compensation for this current disorder and upheaval.

Seoras: Does it no strike ye that it's really no what the Estate can get out o the diggings but more what the Estate can do til alleviate the wants an sorrows o a starving population?

Peacock: I am getting rather tired of you telling me how to run the Estate! I remind you again, that up to now you have been living under the patronage and gratis of His Grace, the Duke. Many other landlords would not even tolerate your presence, let alone these activities!

Seoras: Can ye no at least wait until after the experienced diggers arrive? Then ye'll get what ye're looking for – a professional appraisal o the potential gold yield o the strath. An yer Estate will make money!

Peacock: I repeat, we shall have no mercenaries here! I've made the position of the Estate on that matter quite clear.

Seoras: (*exasperated*) Why? Why? Why?

Meg: Calm yersel, Seoras. Mister Peacock must do what he must do.

Peacock: I'm only implementing His Grace the Duke's wishes.

Sandy: That a fact now?

Peacock: When the date of the implementation of the regulations has been decided upon a detachment of police officers will be stationed here in the camp to see that they are carried out.

Meg: Police officers? But there's never been one wrong deed done here. Not one!

Sandy: There's no one single shebeen the length o Strath Ulliean. Unfortunately.

Meg: An that's the way it'll stay. But police officers! Think o the shame it'll bring.

Peacock: Unfortunately, it's the law, Mrs Mackay.

Sandy: The law, the law! Ye'll be telling me next that the Sheriff himsel'll be taking up lodgings here.

Peacock stares Sandy in the face with just a hint of menace.

Peacock: That's not such a wayward suggestion.

Sandy: Weel, I doubt if he'll come. I hear he's a bit too fond o the craitur til tolerate our temperate ways.

Peacock: Your breath tells me a different story. *(he makes to leave)* Well, I think that's everything. If you wish to see me about anything at all you can find me in my office in Dunrobin. Good day to you.

He turns to the audience; the other actors freeze.

Oh I know how I appear in your eyes. I know, I *do* know. The evil factor harassing an already oppressed people. But am I to blame for the propensity of history? Would it surprise you if I told you that I too wish prosperity to come again to Strath Ulliean? It may also surprise you to know that I have no real liking for the aristocrat and the landowner. They spend their rents like minor kings with little thought for the following year. I am a manager of land and yet I am not free to manage. The princes of leisure, as they sport among the hils, turn their noses up in contempt at my husbandry. And yet the people hate *me*, not them. They'll doff their caps and tug their forelocks all too readily for Lord and Lady Whoever. The very same gentry who cleared them. But it's *my* face they see. It is *my* name they know, miscall and despise. For I am their factor. But I ask no pity from you, for what good is that to me? No. I just wish you to know who I am. I am a man. A man who has a job to do. That is all I am.

There is a short silence as it all sinks in; the other actors come back to life.

Meg: There's no much hope in that man.

Sandy: No for us, anyroads. *(he takes a fly swig from his flask)*

Catriona: *(as if it has just occurred to her)* It's as if we're in the way. But there's nothing here, no any more.

Sandy: An that's the way they want it. An empty strath is a place free o trouble. For men like Peacock we're just trouble.

Meg: Every time we see a factor there's trouble.

Sandy: But factors be damned! This is our land! My grandfather's buried here. An his father, an his father afore him. What's Peacock til Strath Ulliean? A usurper, a... a...

Catriona: *(coldly)* A factor. That's what he is. Our future is no their future. More pity on us.

Meg: That's a stony view, lassie, an one that's aye plagued us. But the like o Mister Peacock willna endure. No Duke, nor palace neither. But Ulliean will endure. But like I say, it's a stony view. *(pause)* Now Sandy Grant, I've a job for ye. My hut's arrived an no matter what the factor says it's going til go up. The diggers need a shop, do they no? I've got a laddie from Wick til give ye a hand. He seems a fine

Seoras and Catriona

Seoras and Catriona pan for gold

enough loon but ye can never tell with a Gallagh*. Ye canna understand what they say half the time.

Sandy: They dinna have the Gàidhlig, poor souls. Just that clackin Scots tongue. It's like the skraik o a hen.

Sandy and Meg laugh and make to go.

Sandy: An dinna fash so, Seoras. It's a long road that doesna bend. We'll see a way through this. We can pool our resources. That'll see a few staying here, at any rate. Look on the bright side, boy; Ye've said yersel that there's too many on the same burns. Maybe this'll make a few explore a bit further?

Seoras: Maybe so, I just canna think straight the now.

Catriona: Ye heard Peacock, Sandy. Three burns only.

Meg: It's rest ye need, Seoras. Ye've been too hard at it of late. The morn, who knows, it'll all seem different. Now, Sandy, stop dithering an we'll go.

Sandy: It's a good hot toddy I'm needing.

Meg: (*shooing him off*) Toddy? I'll give ye toddy!

Sandy and Meg exit. Catriona moves nearer to Seoras.

Catriona: (*softly*) Ye mustna take it all so personally, Seoras. They're right. We can work something out. We must.

Seoras: (*as if in a dream*) Between this (*he stares at his left hand*) an this (*he does likewise with right*) falls nothing.

Catriona: (*in gentle annoyance*) Seoras.

Seoras: Til this New Zealand seems like a paradise.

He turns to her. Meanwhile Aslief has entered. Music gently stirs and reaches a climax by the end of the scene.

Seoras: I want these diggings til work. Damn it, Catriona, there's gold here aplenty if only we had the peace til work it. We've cleared a few hundred pounds already. Peedee Sinclair says he'll buy whatever we find. He may be a bit o a crook but he's no fool in that regard. We can syndicate with him an cut out all the fly boys with the weighted scales. The factor's no friend til the jeweller either.

Catriona: Then we can petition. We can organise. Peacock's decrees canna be legal.

Seoras: I'm no politician. I'm a gold digger. That's all I know. Bickering with factors an lawyers just isna my style. Anyway the Duke's money'll shout the loudest in any courtroom we find oursels in.

Catriona: But we must try. Otherwise there's no point til anything!

Seoras: Why has it got til be this? Och I so wanted til get away from the hungry chaos we've had up until now. Then ruin comes. A ruin called Peacock.

Catriona: When we set off from Otago we didna expect it til be easy.

---

*The natives of Sutherland are known as Caitach (Cattachs); they call Caithness folk Gallagh.

Seoras: Expect? Expect? I didna expect it til be impossible! An is it so wrong til expect a *small* something? We should return til New Zealand, Catriona, for our agreement didna foresee this.

Catriona: If we leave now, an bury the thought, we leave beaten, unended, like a broken hoop.

Seoras: At least in Otago we had our freedom.

Catriona moves across stage. Aslief moves in opposite direction.

Catriona: Freedom, oh freedom, when ever have folk like us been free?

Seoras: Then what point is there til all this?

Catriona: Alright. Seoras, ye go back til New Zealand! Go back til the Otago river! Find gold there again! Ye're so good at it. An when ye look on it ye'll be lookin alone, unless ye can find someone else, for I'll no be there til share yer glory.

Seoras: But our bargain. Ye said...

Catriona: I said if we found gold. We've found gold alright, but it's no in the ground. It's here, deep inside us. Dinna cancel out what's good in yersel by wastin it on what's bad in Sutherland. On the long journey o our love, Seoras, I am a volunteer. There's ower enough weakness in me til tolerate it in ye. If ye fall, then I'll withdraw. For ye've been a part o my life ever since I was a little girl. If ye stop now, I'm alone.

Seoras: Then ye hev doubts too? Surely no ye?

Catriona: What d'ye think I am? Can ye no see the fear in my eyes? Have I grown intil such a stranger til ye that ye canna see that?

Seoras: Forgive me, Catriona, I see it now.

Catriona: Then love that too. Oh Seoras, I want ye in my life the strong man that ye are. I want the energy an purpose that's in ye, but I want it here. If ye go back til New Zealand it'll all go. Ye'll be a dead man. Hunger and Want can plague the soul jsut as well as they weaken the body.

Seoras: Then let our weakness be our strength. From darkness til daylight is a short journey really.

Catriona: Likewise from ice til fire. Ye an me, Seoras, we're like two birds an could fly as freely.

Aslief: For we have wings
that if we fall
greater than
our rise shall be
O Strath Ulliean
O golden

The two women continue to circle each other.

Catriona: But we are as birds
for we migrate like them
We travel the world

an in all its four corners
our tongue is spoken
Aslief: Canada
New Zealand
Australia
America
O Strath Ulliean
O golden
Catriona: An like the birds
our strength is our number
like them our purpose
is our travel
Our lives are only
a gathering
Aslief: Then gather now
your pick
your sail
Gather now
your pan
your keel
Gather now
your hopes
your dreams

> ***Catriona** grasps **Aslief**'s hand triumphantly.*

Catriona: O Strath Ulliean
O golden!

> *Music into next scene.*

Scene Three

*The scene is still that of Baile an Or. Music is heard. It is the
same, thematically, as that heard in Act I Scene 4 when **Hunger**
and **Want** first made their appearance. They appear now,
crossing the stage in sinister fashion. **Seoras** and **Sinclair** are
standing some space apart, staring out at the audience. **Hunger**
and **Want** eventually exit.*

Seoras: Damn it all til hell, we have rights! We canna be tied til three
burns an taxed short o slavery!

Sinclair: If you told a man he could make a sovereign by mending
boots, or by some other dull task, he would go reluctantly to his
work, would he not? But if you told him he could pick that same
sovereign out of the ground he would delve and dig for far more
hours than it would take him to make his boots. No? I know this, for
I am a jeweller. Delight, ladies and gentlemen, sweetens toil.

Seoras: The Duke earns over one hundred thousand pounds a year
from his Estate. What he takes from us is a drop in the ocean, but it's
our length and breadth. If he must milk us then ten shillings a month,
or less, would be acceptable. We work, we toil. But we gain nothing.

Sinclair: I pay three pounds ten shillings per ounce for all the gold
brought to me. I am not a bad man… just careful. Some rogues are
offering three pounds eight shillings per ounce. Scoundrels. For the
sake of my fellow man and for the good of all I buy all they have off
them for three pounds eight and sixpence. Like I say, I'm not a bad
man… just careful.

Seoras: The digging is all but exhausting me. If I could sink a shaft under
the burn then I'd be getting somewhere. I've selected the site. Everything tells me this is where the gold stream has flowed down off the
higher quartz rocks. But I need permission. An so far it hasna come.

Sinclair: Most of the local diggers are leaving the scene now. The Lewis
fishings have started and they seem to prefer risking their lives
hunting fish in the Minch to turning the sod in search of gold. Well,
each to his own. Mainly, now, the prospectors are colonials invited
here by Mister Mackay. I do so enjoy dealing with men of experience
and knowledge. Of course once they were here Mister Peacock had
no option but to allow them access. Profits, sadly, are down. But
expectations, on the other hand, are up. If the stuff is going to be
found in any rewarding quantities then these colonials are the boys
to find it. And Peter Dominicus Sinclair is their friend. Sincerely.

Seoras: We're tied til our claims for a month. We canna move if the
stretch isna paying. Many are disgruntled. The system, they say, is
reducing them til poverty. One pound a week isna enough for men
that are used to earning five pounds, or even a hundred pounds a
week, in Australia and New Zealand. More than that, the spirit is
leaving Strath Ulliean.

Sinclair: My feelings on the matter are this: the mining regulations are far too illiberal and antiquated. Consequently the diggers are severely confined. Nothing has been achieved here except that they have made a beginning. I want to buy another shop! And, ladies and gentlemen, how can I on three burns? These landlords seem to want to prolong the century. Well, I say end it now…
"Ill fares the land, to hastening ills a-prey.
Where wealth accumulates and men decay."
A jeweller needs his diggers. Amen to that. Yes.

> *Seoras turns and addresses Sinclair.*

Seoras: Peedee, I have here something I think'll interest ye.

Sinclair: Yes, and what is that, pray tell?

Seoras: A nugget, Peedee. One an a half ounces if she's a dram!

> *Seoras hands Sinclair the nugget and he peers at it through his lens.*

Sinclair: My, my, my! A very handsome metal., Mister Mackay, very handsome indeed.

Seoras: I thought ye'd like it.

Sinclair: And where about did you discover it exactly? Or is that a secret? Oh, I know you diggers. Ethical code, all that sort of thing.

Seoras: Och it's no secret, Peedee, no til ye anyway. The Suisgill, that's where she came from. An there's more like her. But ye can keep that under yer hat.

Sinclair: The Suisgill, the Suisgill. A beautifully rich name, don't you think? Suisgill, Suisgill. As to your request, my word is my bond, Mister Mackay. A jeweller has to be an honest man.

Seoras: Of course, of course. I believe ye. (*aside*) Though thousands wouldna.

Sinclair: We are a misunderstood breed, an there's no getting away from that. The jeweller's curse, Mister Mackay, the jeweller's curse.

Seoras: I need til sink a mine shaft. I need til get under the burn til the seam itsel.

Sinclair: An for this you'll be needing capital, yes?

Seoras: Exactly. It would be a good investment.

Sinclair: And I suppose you want me to lend you this capital, no?

Seoras: Weel, I dinna expect the Duke til cough up.

Sinclair: The Sutherland Estate wishes to end the gold diggings here in Strath Ulliean. You must be aware of that, Mister Mackay.

Seoras: It had crossed my mind.

Sinclair: You see, many eyes look upon these proceedings. The Duke of Portland, for example, looks at them down the barrel of a gun. His posse roams the hillsides on the borders of his estate.

Seoras: There's gold in all these hills. The Scarabens are made o quartz. I would say diamonds could be found, for those with eyes til see.

Sinclair: Diamonds! Diamonds, you say? Are you sure?

Seoras: Ye canna be sure o anything in this game, Peedee. But I know my business. I came here looking for gold, weel, ye hold it in yer hand.

Sinclair: Indeed, indeed. But let me tell you this again: Peacock wants these diggings ended. Some of your diggers harbour curious notions. Curious to Mister Peacock at least.

Seoras: Aside from foreigners they're Cattachs* mostly. What they feel they state in actions.

Sinclair: But that's the problem exactly. Strath Ulliean was cleared for a reason. Peacock is not happy with the return of the sons and grandsons. Wing, gill and hoof are more manageable and productive than your Cattachs.

Seoras: But I'm producing something! This land is wealthy. Countries that are made out o no more than sand an rock seem til manage better.

Sinclair: You have a great gift, Mister Mackay. Not many men see the world so clearly.

Seoras: I know about gold. There's nothing fancy in that. But a gift is given an I receive it gladly, an with gratitude. But it isna mine alone. It's for everybody, an it can just as easily be taken back.

Sinclair: Oh, you Celts. What notions... what notions! I tell you this, Baile an Or will be razed to the ground. All these tents and huts will go. You're an embarrassment, Mister Mackay, and history is a cruel and ruthless beast. For fifty years this strath has been given over to sheep and deer. Why should the Estate want to change that state of affairs? But what do I know? I'm only a jeweller.

Seoras: Ye benefit by our labours, d'ye no?

Sinclair: Handsomely, handsomely. In that regard I have no complaints. But there is nothing I can do for you except to give you money. And money, I fear, is not much good to you at present.

> *Enter **Aslief** and **Catriona**. Music rises gently. The men are unaware of the women.*

Seoras: (*angrily*) But this place *can* work! The gold *is* here! I'm here! What on God's earth is til stop us?

Sinclair: I will tell you again: the Sutherland Estate. Are you both deaf and blind?

Catriona: Dinna be so obsessive, Seoras. We can find gold in other straths.

Aslief: His heart is on fire.

Seoras: The people can live an prosper in this strath. We know what til do now. We know what til give, an what til take!

Sinclair: I'm sympathetic to your cause, believe me. But you'll never win by confrontation. The frontal charge lies dead and buried as an

---

*People of the Cait, or Cat in English: Sutherlanders.

idea upon Culloden Field. And besides, the herring fishing will recover and most of your Cattachs will go back to them. Why, they're going now! There's gold in the sea now, Mister Mackay. You have a rival in her.

Seoras: The sea, the sea! All I hear is talk o the sea, the sea an the price o herring!

Aslief: I hear the music of choking lungs
ancient voices speak to us

Sinclair: But there is much money to be made. There's curing. Barrelling. Exports to the Baltic, even Jamaica! It's the modern world, Mister Mackay, the modern world.

Seoras: Then herring be damned! We're no natural seamen. It's the land we're from!

Sinclair: Oh, the hills and glens. I forgot about them. The hills and glens.

Aslief: A man must hold his head high
but he must also know the world.

Catriona: Come home til me, Seoras
for the day is growing old
the night is wearing her dark face (*exit Catriona*)

Seoras: Why can I no turn my hand til my craft in a place I know as home?

Aslief: Many call Ulliean mother
many call her bitch an viper

Sinclair: I suggest you make the best of it. Settle up. Forget these gold diggings as I myself sadly must.

Seoras: I willna! I canna!

Sinclair: Like I say, Mister Mackay, what do I know about it? I am only a humble jeweller. (*he looks at the nugget and slyly slips it into his pocket*) Hills and glens, hills and glens. But now, unfortunately, I must return to my shop. Urgent matters await me. I'm sure you understand. Good day, Mister Mackay. I'm almost positive you have no idea of how much I wish you well. But be careful. Struggle is a dangerous business. And jailers are hungry men. (*he moves off*) Ah me. Hills and glens, hills and glens.

Seoras: (*shouting after him*) An I hope yer customers are happy! Is that all it's come down til? Mere ornamentation? (*he buries his head in his hands*) Brooches? What use is it?

*Music swells. **Aslief** moves across stage to **Seoras** much as she did at their first meeting.*

Aslief: Deep are riches hidden
an hard is honour's path
in the heart
or in the strath
we must do
as we are bidden

O Strath Ulliean
O golden

Tomorrow is an eagle
high upon the mountain
an gold is a dream
that bears no counting
for we are much more
than we seem
O Strath Ulliean
O golden

The music fades a little but continues as they speak:

Alone again, Seoras? Or at least ye think ye are?

Seoras: (*looking up at her impatiently*) It's ye again, spey-wife. Hev ye come til gloat?

Aslief: Ye can cry me what ye will. Spey-wife, Feeach, Witch. They've all come my way afore now.

Seoras: No doubt.

Aslief: But I never gloat. I just notice.

Seoras: Well, what hev ye noticed?

Aslief: That ye're tired. But ye're no alone.

Seoras: Ye're right enough there, Mistress, for I've two hundred gold diggers waiting on me til resolve their predicament.

Aslief: I see that.

Seoras: Then ye see plenty.

Aslief: But I see more, much more.

Seoras: Then maybe ye see a way out o this fiddle?

Aslief: Maybe I do.

Seoras: Then tell me, for it seems I canna move in any way at all!

Aslief: Oh but ye can, Seoras, ye can.

Seoras: How? Tell me, for Mercy's sake!

Aslief: By standing up, for a start.

He does so, almost automatically and despite himself.

Aslief: An by moving forward in yer mind.

Seoras: My mind is weary. I need til rest.

Aslief: Ôh, ye'll sleep soon enough, my strong bouyag, in a clay cradle behind the sun, in the land o song.

Seoras: Riddles, why is it always riddles?

Aslief: Because it is life, an meaning holds til no boundaries, no estate or kingdoms.

*Enter a modern **miner**, dressed in overalls, hardhat, lamp etc.*

Aslief: (*to Seoras*) Here is someone ye know well. Someone who at present is in your imagination.

Seoras: What d'ye mean? His clothes, his helmet, they're strange indeed, although his face is familiar. But I've never met him afore. (*to the* *miner*) Excuse me, my friend, but this woman conjures visions out o thin air. I'd be wary o her if I was ye.

*The **miner** does not answer.*

Seoras: (*to **Aslief***) Why does he no speak? Has he no tongue?

Aslief: No Gaelic, but Scots, an it's asleep unless I loosen it. For he is dreaming this from a time far distant from us, over the space that a hundred years canna fill.

Seoras: Ye mean...? (*to the **miner***) Look, man, just who are ye?

Miner: I am Macleod, Mackay an Bannerman. I am Sutherland, Keith, Calder an Gunn. I am Miller, Macdonald, Ross an Mackenzie. Henderson, Manson, Swanson, Sinclair an Nicholson. I am the North.

Seoras: (*to **Aslief***) The man's havering, for he says he is no one person.

Aslief: But look, Seoras, an listen harder. For he is you.

Seoras: Me? But I'm here now. Time's are hard enough without this, this...

Aslief: Time. Time, my gold digger, is a poem. Time is a song, a necessary fiction.

Seoras: Look, I'm a simple man. All this I dinna understand.

Aslief: Then ye're no different from yer future self. He too is a gold digger.

Seoras: (*to the **miner***) Then ye work here in Strath Ulliean? Or are ye over in Caithness?

Miner: I am gold digger, miner, fisherman and crofter. I am roughneck, roustabout an derrickman. I am joiner, electrician, mason, baker an butcher. I sail, I farm, I build.

Seoras: Then ye're a magician as weel, friend. (*to **Aslief***) Ye say he's asleep?

Aslief: Only in dreams do we truly travel. Only in our dreams are we really free. But this man's work is no different from yours. His labour is as honest as your own.

Seoras: Then the diggings'll continue here? The gold field'll succeed? Is that what you're saying?

Aslief: I am saying what I have been telt til say. Ulliean'll no let her children go down that easily. Yer struggle here, Seoras, is a brave one, but it is only a small part of a greater pattern. Yer father lies now closer til gold than ye'll ever know. Yer sons an grandsons aside him.

Seoras: Stop these riddles. I canna thole them!

Aslief: They belong til the land an the land belongs til them. An they, an you, an the land'll endure. These are ancient ties an canna be broken. Before ye is yerself, an the shape o yer success.

Miner: I have bread an herring. I have barley an meal, meat an drink. Oil, gas an gold.

Seoras: Gold? Gold, ye say?

Miner: Beneath burn an river. Beneath mountain an seabed. I have gold. I have your name.

*He holds out his hand in greeting. **Seoras** takes it, despite himself.*

Seoras: What sort o sorcery is this? Yer voice is strange, my friend, but yer grip is firm enough.

Aslief: Our words are runes carved on stone by the wind.

***Seoras** finishes shaking hands and stares at his palm in disbelief. There is a large nugget in it.*

Seoras: A good size nugget! Five ounces, I would guess. Where did you find this, friend? Was it the Suisgill? Or the Ulliean herself?

Miner: In all the burns, in all the straths. In highland, lowland, island an firth.

Seoras: (*to the **miner***) Then there's hope here?

Aslief: An power.

***Seoras** turns to **Aslief**. Exit the **miner**.*

Seoras: An gold?

Aslief: Yes, gold. There is always gold. For the people.

Seoras: But how can I make it work?

Aslief: By awakening. By imagination. By moving forward.

***Seoras** turns to address the **miner**, who has left.*

Seoras: Yer nugget, *a bhalaich***, it's... (*to **Aslief***) Where has he gone?

Aslief: To rejoin his sleep. To his song, his dream.

Seoras: (*confused*) So did I dream him then?

Aslief: We are all dream. We are all the children o dream.

*Enter **Catriona**.*

Catriona: Be still now, *a gràidh*†. My arms are a harbour for ye. Let me kiss ye intil the still dawn. Come rock with me, my golden boy.

***Seoras** crosses to her and they embrace.*

Seoras: We hev gold, Catriona, real gold. An they canna take it off us. No with regulations, with licences nor police!

Catriona: The world is ours. Together we're as much gold as the world can bear.

*Enter **Meg**, **Bridei** and **Broath***

Meg: Ye can take the people out o the strath but ye can never take the strath out o the people.

Seoras: (*to **Catriona**, as if gaining inner strength*) Then we'll have til pan for other things!

Catriona: Bigger things!

Aslief: The night has no hold upon
the morning

Meg: (*to **Seoras***) A force o police are on their way here from Tain. Helmsdale's full o it.

---

*My friend.
†My love.

Seoras: The Baile an Or is done for?

Catriona: Let them have it. For what is it? Nothing.

Meg: A dry stretch o river bed. A silent hill.

Aslief: A story o serpents and kings
     an history

Catriona: (*to Seoras*) The digging o gold is the continuation o poverty
     by other means.

Meg: (*to Catriona*) The struggle here now, although we lose it, means
     our winning is no far at hand.

Aslief: Gold is the basic star
     in the universe o greed
     it has false light
     an knows no echo
     it tempts with joy
     an pays in sorrow

Meg: O Strath Ulliean
     O golden

Seoras: (*joyfully, after breaking free from Catriona*) Then put fire til
     everything!

     Broath and Bridei now act out the destruction of Baile an Or.

Catriona: Til tent an shake-up!

Meg: Til hut an stall!

Seoras: Til bunk-beds an blankets!

Catriona: Til sleep itsel!

Aslief: Til the tears o Broath!

     Broath freezes.

Aslief: Til Bridei's teeth!

     Bridei freezes.

Aslief: Here now a golden fury
     upon the water
     here now a silence
     along the strath

     Gold is the cradle o the moon
     an the necklace o the sun
     an gold will be here
     when both moon an sun are done

     for our tale is told
     an hereby ended

     O Strath Ulliean
     O golden.

     Music finishes.

The End